red hot and green

red hot and green

50 spicy vegetarian recipes

cooking with chilies, peppercorns, mustards, horseradish, and ginger

by Janet Hazen

photography by Joyce Oudkerk Pool

CHRONICLE BOOKS

SAN FRANCISCO

Library of Congress Cataloging-in-Publication Data:
Hazen, Janet.
Red, hot, and green : 50 spicy vegetarian recipes : cooking with chilies,
peppercorns, mustards, horseradish, and ginger / by Janet Hazen ;
photography by Joyce Oudkerk Pool.
p. cm.
Includes index.
ISBN 0-8118-1052-6
1. Vegetarian cookery. 2. Cookery, International. 3. Spices. I. Title.
TX837.H423 1996
641.5'636—dc20   95-31835   CIP

Design by: Rachel O'Dowd
Author photo by: Joyce Oudkerk Pool

Printed in Hong Kong

Distributed in Canada by
Raincoast Books, 8680 Cambie St., Vancouver, B.C. V6P 6M9

10 9 8 7 6 5 4 3 2 1

Chronicle Books
275 Fifth Street
San Francisco, CA 94103

Dedication ➤ ➤ ➤   *This book is dedicated to Father Bernie Bush, S.J., spiritual advisor, friend, and angel in human form.*

First thanks go to my family, Irene, Bruce, and Jennifer, for their unfailing support, patience, and love. To Jackie, Joan, Lisa, Julie, Cindi, Fred, Kim, and Evelyn—you will be forever in my heart.

Much appreciation to Bill LeBlond, Leslie Jonath, and the staff at Chronicle Books for their work on this book.

To a diligent and ever-perceptive editor, Carolyn Krebs, my gratitude for yet another wonderful job.

Many thanks to Pouke, for her elegant and effortless food styling, and to Joyce, for her magnificent photography.

CONTENTS

15

ginger

33

mustard

55

peppercorns

75

horseradish

93

chilies

INTRODUCTION

In two previous books, *Hot, Hotter, Hottest* and *Turn It Up!*, I singed my palate exploring the culinary possibilities of five ingredients with varying amounts of firepower: ginger, mustard, peppercorns, horseradish, and chili peppers. Using these favorite foods as inspiration, I have turned up the heat once again to create this volume of vegetarian recipes.

Ginger, mustard, peppercorns, horseradish, and chilies are all wonderful flavor boosters, and it's only natural that these ingredients would star in a vegetarian cookbook. Although their bold tastes are favored by omnivores as well, these fiery staples supply flavor "insurance" in dishes that do not rely on meat, poultry, fish, or seafood for their flavor.

Not so very long ago, vegetarian cooking in this country was synonymous in people's minds with leaden grain breads, artless salads piled high with sprouts, and tasteless casseroles made with meat substitutes; it was not the realm of the true gourmand. But we have come a long way in the past decade, in large part due to the influence of ethnic cuisines that traditionally have included little or no meat but are nonetheless flavorful and satisfying. Immigrants from Southeast Asia, India, China, Latin America, and many other countries, along with a proliferation of cookbooks featuring their cuisines, have greatly expanded our sense of the creative possibilities of vegetarian cookery. The recipes in this book reflect this worldly influence; from classics to newly developed dishes, they encircle the globe in origin and essence.

Although many people choose to be vegetarians for philosophical reasons, the growing trend in low-fat, high-fiber eating makes vegetarian fare all the more appealing to those of us concerned with our health. Dishes made without meat, poultry, fish, and seafood are often very low in fat and high in required nutrients. Although some recipes in this book are prepared with heavy cream, butter, and cheese, these ingredients are usually used in modest amounts, and most dishes fall under the heading of moderate to low in fat. To my mind, this healthfulness is an added bonus, not an end in itself; all of these recipes have so much flavor, body, texture, and visual interest, they will appeal to everyone, even if you still eat some meat and fish.

My wish is that both vegetarians and nonvegetarians will find comfort and inspiration in this collection of recipes. I also hope that you discover something new, something exciting, and something very delicious to spark your palate.

FROM SOUP TO NUTS

STOCKING YOUR PANTRY: In addition to the flavor arsenal provided by chilies, ginger, horseradish, mustard, and peppercorns, which are discussed in the chapter introductions, there are a few commercially prepared items I find vital to vegetarian cookery. Chinese mushroom soy sauce, Japanese miso, and Italian or domestic dried mushrooms can be used to add intense flavor and body to soups, stews, sauces, dressings, and sautéed dishes. They can heighten the taste of most any dish without adding fat; their bold characteristics help take the place of meat or poultry in a vegetarian dish.

To provide flexibility in creating new dishes and to make many of the recipes in this book, you will find it very useful to have the following ingredients on hand: regular soy sauce (some folks also use tamari sauce); black and regular rice wine vinegar; balsamic, red wine, and champagne or white wine vinegars; peanut, vegetable, and olive oils; canned tomatoes, tomato paste in a tube, and sun-dried tomatoes; an assortment of dried and canned beans; a variety of grains such as cracked wheat, cornmeal, barley, buckwheat, and jasmine and wild rice; and several different kinds of dried pasta.

In my refrigerator I also try to stock jars of Chinese hot black bean, chili, hoisin, and plum sauces; a variety of domestic and imported olives; assorted nuts and nut butters; imported Parmesan cheese (chunk form—not pregrated); and Asian sesame oil. Armed with these staples, you can make a nutritious and flavor-packed grain or pasta dish in just minutes. You won't have any excuse for bland or boring dishes coming from your kitchen with a battery of such potent-tasting condiments. Even prepared foods can be doctored to a palatable state using one or two of these ingredients.

TAKING STOCK: For vegetarian cookery, one of the most important staples to have on hand is good-quality vegetable stock, for which I have included a basic recipe (following). You can use it to make soups and stews; to make sauces or dressings; to add to sautéed vegetables; or for cooking grains. When you make a pot of homemade vegetable stock, you may want to double the recipe so that you can freeze some for later use. You'll find it very convenient to have varying sizes of containers of the frozen stock in your freezer to thaw as needed for cooking.

If you're pressed for time, a good alternative is canned vegetable broth, a marvelous new product. Although both regular and low-sodium varieties contain hefty doses of sodium compared to homemade stock, they are an invaluable time-saver for last-minute cooking.

vegetable stock

➤ Use the basic stock that follows in recipes that call for homemade vegetable stock. I have suggested ingredients based on seasonal vegetables, but you can experiment with a variety of fresh or slightly wilted vegetables, depending on what you have in your refrigerator. Avoid using eggplant, potatoes, and large amounts of celery leaves and bell peppers, however, as these ingredients can make the stock bitter and give it an "off" taste.

Although the two ingredient lists ("Fall and Winter"; "Spring and Summer") allow the cook to take advantage of seasonal vegetables to prepare stock, either list produces a rich-tasting, full-bodied vegetable stock suitable for use in any of the recipes in this book.

makes about 4 quarts

Place the vegetables (and peppercorns, for Fall and Winter Stock) in a 12-quart, heavy-bottomed pot and sweat over high heat 3 to 4 minutes, stirring frequently, until they are warm and aromatic. Add 6 quarts of the water and bring to a boil. Reduce the heat to moderate and simmer 2 hours, stirring occasionally. Add the remaining water and cook 1½ hours. Strain through a colander and discard the solids. Strain a second time through a fine wire sieve. Cool to room temperature. Transfer to a container with a tight-fitting lid and store in the refrigerator for up to 4 days or in smaller containers in the freezer for up to 3 months.

FALL AND WINTER VEGETABLE STOCK:

3 large onions, coarsely chopped

½ small winter squash, coarsely chopped

4 medium carrots, coarsely chopped

4 stalks celery, coarsely chopped

16 mushrooms, quartered

3 medium zucchini, coarsely chopped

½ pound green beans, coarsely chopped

2 large tomatoes, coarsely chopped

1 head garlic, smashed

1½ tablespoons black peppercorns

9 quarts cold water

SPRING AND SUMMER VEGETABLE STOCK:

2 large onions, coarsely chopped

3 bunches scallions, coarsely chopped

2 medium carrots, coarsely chopped

2 stalks celery, coarsely chopped

3 medium zucchini, coarsely chopped

2 ears corn, cut into five sections

2 large tomatoes, coarsely chopped

½ pound green beans, coarsely chopped

½ pound asparagus, coarsely chopped

½ pound snow or sugar snap peas, coarsely chopped

6 cloves garlic

9 quarts cold water

ginger

◆ ◆ ◆ ◆ ◆   **GINGER**

Ginger is an ingredient most often associated with Asian cooking, especially Chinese, Vietnamese, and Thai. The warm, tingling, sometimes sharp flavor of fresh ginger enhances the flavors and textures of other traditional ingredients used in these cuisines. Ginger ought not be limited to just Asian food, however. As the recipes in this chapter will show, ginger can add sparkle and gentle heat to a wide variety of dishes, from appetizers to desserts.

This chapter opens with a warm, inviting conserve made from sweet caramelized shallots, dried figs, and fresh ginger—a versatile and delicious condiment. In the *Spiced Ginger, Pear, and Tomato Relish,* fresh ginger marries with juicy pears and savory tomatoes to form a marvelous sweet-savory relish that can be used with scrambled or poached eggs or as a spread for grilled cheese sandwiches.

In salads, the unique, fresh flavor of ginger is particularly appealing. It provides the perfect foil for fresh mint in the *Apple-Carrot Slaw with Ginger-Mint Dressing,* a bright and invigorating salad with a Southeast Asian flavor. In the *Gingered Beet and Fennel Salad,* however, it blends with more traditional Western ingredients to create a soft and subtle flavor.

In addition to several recipes that can be either side dishes or main courses—depending on what they are served with—I also have provided three tempting desserts, including my favorite—*Ginger-Glazed Yam Cakes with Raisins and Walnuts.*

Although referred to as a "root," ginger is actually a rhizome, or underground stem, that grows best when planted in rich, sandy soil in hot, humid climates. Hawaii, Fiji, the Caribbean, Costa Rica, Guatemala, Nicaragua, Australia, India, and China are the primary growers of fresh ginger; China and India are the biggest producers and exporters of powdered ginger, a form used primarily for baked goods and in beverages. Crystallized ginger is usually eaten as a candy or as an after-dinner palate refresher, but it is also used for decorating and garnishing baked goods and other confections. Vinegared ginger is a mainstay of Japanese cuisine, most often paired with sushi or sashimi.

When purchasing fresh ginger, look for very hard roots with smooth, unblemished, light brown skin; the "hand," as the root is often called, should not yield to finger pressure and ought to be free of cuts or dents. Like other fresh produce, it's best to use ginger as soon as possible, but if you need to store it, wrap it tightly in plastic wrap and store in the vegetable bin of your refrigerator. Stored in this manner, fresh ginger will retain its flavor and texture for up to two weeks. It can be stored longer with some success, but rhizomes long past their prime are dry and flavorless.

When eating or cooking with fresh ginger, always remove the outer skin; exceptions to this principle include recipes in which ginger is used for flavoring only and removed at the end of cooking. Young ginger, which is less common in markets, does not require peeling since the skin is very thin and mild tasting and therefore edible.

To peel ginger: Using a sharp paring knife, carefully remove the tough, outer layer of light brown skin and discard. If you are using the entire "hand," first remove the nubs or branches to facilitate peeling.

To cut ginger into slivers: Peel the root and cut across at an angle to produce oval shapes about ⅛ inch thick. Lay the flat oval shapes on the cutting board so that they barely overlap. Cutting the long way on the oval, slice into very thin, long pieces.

To dice ginger: Peel the root and slice one very thin piece from one side. Lay the root on the cutting board on the flat, cut side. Slice the root lengthwise: ⅛ inch wide for very small dice, ¼ inch wide for medium dice, and ½ inch wide for large dice. Stack the slices of ginger and cut again lengthwise into the desired-size strips. Make the final cuts by slicing across into the appropriate-size dice.

To grate ginger: Peel the root and grate on a metal grater. Use the finest setting if you want mostly juice, medium for some pulp and a little juice, and the jumbo or coarsest setting for small bits of the root.

A food processor may also be used to chop, mince, or purée fresh ginger. If the recipe calls for peeled ginger, peel the root before placing it in the food processor. Process using the on/off switch, until the root is the desired size. This method is recommended for recipes that call for coarsely or finely chopped ginger, or minced ginger. To purée the root, use a small amount of liquid such as water, fruit juice, wine, sherry, or soy sauce—whatever liquid is compatible with the recipe you are using.

The circumference of ginger roots can be as thick as a silver dollar and as narrow as a nickel, but most roots are about the thickness of a quarter. The recipes in this book specify amounts in length measurements, and since this isn't exact, following are yields in standard cup measures for varying lengths of an average-size ginger root when finely chopped. You really don't have to use exact measurements of ginger, but some cooks feel better with specific guidelines.

2-inch piece ginger root = about 3 tablespoons, finely chopped

4-inch piece ginger root = about ½ cup, finely chopped

6-inch piece ginger root = about ⅔ cup, finely chopped

8-inch piece ginger root = about 1 cup, finely chopped

caramelized shallot, fig, and ginger conserve

In a large, nonstick shallow-sided saucepan, cook the shallots in the butter and peanut oil over moderately low heat 20 to 25 minutes, stirring occasionally, until golden brown and very soft. Add the figs, ginger, sherry, and water and bring to a boil over high heat, stirring frequently. Reduce the heat to moderately low and cook 20 minutes, stirring occasionally, until figs are tender and mixture is thick and aromatic.

Remove from heat and cool to room temperature before serving or storing. Will keep in a tightly sealed container in the refrigerator for up to 3 weeks.

➤ Spread this sweet-spicy condiment on bread or crackers and serve with slivers of Cheddar or blue cheese. You may also add it to cooked rice, pasta, or grains to add zest, body, and flavor.

HOT 3

makes about 1 ½ cups

8 large shallots, peeled and quartered

1 ½ tablespoons unsalted butter

1 tablespoon peanut or vegetable oil

8 ounces dried Calimyrna figs, stemmed and quartered

4-inch piece fresh ginger root, peeled, quartered, and thinly sliced crosswise

½ cup dry sherry

½ cup water

spiced ginger, pear, and tomato relish

In a large sauté pan, cook the pears, tomatoes, ginger, and spices over high heat 3 minutes, stirring constantly. Add 1 cup of the water and 2 tablespoons of the honey and cook 15 minutes, stirring frequently, until liquid has almost evaporated. Add remaining cup water, remaining 2 tablespoons honey, and the salt. Cook 10 minutes, stirring frequently, until the liquid has evaporated and mixture is thick and soft. Remove from heat and cool to room temperature before storing. Store in a tightly sealed container in the refrigerator for up to 3 weeks.

➤ At once sweet, savory, and prickly with heat, this lively condiment is terrific served with grilled vegetables, baked winter squash, or braised eggplant. This relish makes an ordinary sandwich extraordinary when spread on whole-wheat bread, topped with Gruyère cheese and placed under the broiler until melted and bubbly.

HOTTER 4

makes about 1 ¼ cups

3 firm but ripe pears, stemmed, cored, and finely chopped

6 Roma tomatoes, cored and finely chopped

4-inch piece fresh ginger root, peeled and finely chopped

1 scant teaspoon *each* ground allspice, cloves, anise seeds, mace, and black pepper

2 cups water

¼ cup honey

Pinch salt

gingered beet and fennel salad

3 large beets, trimmed and halved

¹/₂ cup fresh orange juice

1 ¹/₂ tablespoons sherry vinegar or red wine vinegar

3 tablespoons almond or peanut oil

4-inch piece fresh ginger root, peeled and slivered

1 teaspoon ground coriander

Watercress, for lining plate

2 bulbs fennel, trimmed, cored, and thinly sliced

¹/₃ cup toasted almonds, coarsely chopped, for garnish

➤ You may do some of the preparation for this eye-catching salad a day or two ahead, by marinating the cooked beets in the prepared dressing. Add the fennel and almonds at the last minute, then arrange atop the watercress.

HOT 3

makes about 6 servings

Place beets in a large saucepan and cover with cold water. Bring to a boil over high heat. Reduce the heat to moderately high, cover, and cook 45 to 50 minutes, or until tender when pierced with a fork. Drain well and cool to room temperature. When cool enough to handle, peel and slice into ¼-inch wedges.

To make dressing, in a small bowl combine the orange juice, vinegar, oil, ginger, and coriander; mix well.

Place watercress on a large plate or platter. Arrange beets and fennel atop the watercress, and drizzle with the dressing.

Garnish with the almonds and serve immediately.

gingered tomato essence with tofu silk

Soak the mushrooms in warm water 30 to 40 minutes, or until soft and pliable. Drain well. Rinse under cold running water, removing any grit or sand. Slice into very thin strips and set aside.

In a 4-quart, heavy-bottomed pan, place the tomatoes, ginger, and salt. Cook over high heat, crushing the tomatoes and stirring frequently, 12 or 13 minutes, or until the liquid has evaporated and the mixture is slightly thick. Add the water and sake and bring to a boil. Reduce the heat to moderate and simmer 50 to 55 minutes, stirring occasionally. Strain through a fine wire mesh or sieve one or two times or until no seeds remain.

Return the mixture to the pan, and bring to a boil over high heat. Add the reserved mushrooms and the scallions and cook 5 minutes. Add the tofu and cook 3 minutes. Season with salt and pepper and ladle into serving bowls. Serve immediately.

➤ Your palate may be fooled by the richly robust flavor and voluptuous texture of this surprisingly low-fat Japanese-style soup.

In peak season use fresh tomatoes from your garden or local produce stand; off-season use fresh cherry tomatoes instead.

HOTTER 6

makes 6 to 8 servings

6 dried shiitake mushrooms, stemmed

3 pounds large cherry tomatoes, stemmed

5-inch piece fresh ginger root, peeled and finely chopped

1 teaspoon kosher salt

6 cups water

2 cups sake or dry vermouth

3 scallions, green part only, finely chopped

14 ounces soft tofu (1 block), cut into 1/4-inch cubes

Salt and pepper, to taste

apple-carrot slaw with ginger-mint dressing

3 tablespoons seasoned rice wine vinegar

2 tablespoons peanut oil

2 large Asian pears, cored and slivered

2 medium carrots, peeled and slivered

3-inch piece fresh ginger root, peeled and slivered

2 shallots, thinly sliced

Salt and pepper, to taste

$1/3$ cup finely chopped fresh mint

$1/2$ cup toasted peanuts, coarsely chopped, for garnish

➤ Invigorating, refreshing, and lusty in flavor, this Southeast Asian–style salad is very low in calories and fat yet very satisfying. It can be made completely fat-free by omitting the peanut oil and peanuts.

Asian pears, sometimes called apple–pears, can be found year-round in most upscale produce markets, full-service grocery stores, natural food stores, and Asian markets. If you can't find Asian pears, use slightly underripe European pears such as Bartlett or Anjou; very firm Bosc pears are also an excellent substitute.

HOT 3

makes 4 to 6 servings

In a large bowl, whisk together the vinegar and peanut oil to form a smooth emulsion. Add the pears, carrots, ginger, and shallots; mix gently. Season with salt and pepper. (The salad can be prepared to this point and refrigerated for up to 3 hours.) Just before serving, add the mint and mix gently. Serve immediately, garnished with the peanuts.

braised eggplant with ginger and black beans

3 tablespoons peanut oil

1 tablespoon toasted sesame oil

5 medium Chinese or Italian eggplants, trimmed and cut on the diagonal into 1-inch pieces

5 cloves garlic, finely chopped

5-inch piece fresh ginger root, peeled and thinly sliced

1/2 cup dry sherry or vermouth

3 tablespoons bottled hoisin or plum sauce

2 1/2 tablespoons soy sauce

1 1/2 tablespoons Chinese-style chili–black bean sauce

1 bunch scallions, finely chopped

1/4 cup minced fresh cilantro or sesame seeds, for garnish

➤ To add a delightful crunchy texture to this dish, add about one cup of drained and rinsed water chestnuts along with the scallions. Toss with cooked noodles or serve atop steamed rice. For a cross-cultural salad, serve warm on a bed of mixed baby greens.

All ingredients for this recipe may be purchased in any Asian market and most full-service grocery stores.

HOTTER 6

makes about 4 servings

In a heavy-bottomed shallow saucepan, heat the peanut and sesame oils over moderately high heat until hot but not smoking. Add the eggplant and cook 2 minutes, stirring frequently. Add the garlic and ginger and cook 2 minutes. Add the sherry, hoisin sauce, soy sauce, and chili–black bean sauce and bring to a boil over high heat. Cook 2 minutes, stirring once or twice. Reduce the heat to moderate and cover. Cook 10 to 12 minutes, or until the eggplant is tender but not mushy and the liquids have thickened. Add the scallions and mix gently. Serve immediately, garnished with the cilantro or sesame seeds.

ginger-lemongrass vegetable stir-fry

In a very large, nonstick sauté pan or wok, heat the oil until hot, but not smoking. Add the lemongrass, shallots, garlic, ginger, carrots, and green beans. Cook over high heat 2 minutes, stirring constantly.

Add the lotus root, baby corn, straw mushrooms, fish sauce, sherry, chili paste, and sugar. Cook 2 minutes, stirring constantly, until all vegetables are crisp-tender and sauce is aromatic. Remove from heat. Serve immediately, garnished with the cilantro or basil.

➤ Bright-tasting lemongrass and fresh ginger add sparkle to this colorful Vietnamese stir-fry. For a complete meal, spoon over steamed jasmine rice or toss with cooked noodles.

Asian grocery stores or produce markets and some upscale or natural food stores may carry the ingredients needed for this recipe. If you can't find fresh lotus root, you may use canned instead.

HOTTER 4

makes 4 to 6 servings

2 tablespoons peanut oil

3 stalks lemongrass, trimmed

3 shallots, thinly sliced

3 cloves garlic, finely chopped

4-inch piece fresh ginger root, peeled and thinly sliced

2 medium carrots, slivered

1/2 pound small green beans, trimmed

1/2 fresh lotus root (4 to 5 inches), peeled and thinly sliced

1 can (14 ounces) baby corn or baby bamboo shoots, drained and rinsed

1 can (15 ounces) straw mushrooms, drained and rinsed

3 tablespoons fish sauce (nuoc cham)

2 tablespoons dry sherry

1 1/2 teaspoons Vietnamese or Chinese chili paste

1 teaspoon sugar

1/2 cup finely chopped fresh cilantro or basil, for garnish

ginger-glazed yam cakes with raisins and walnuts

GINGER GLAZE:

2 cups sugar

2 cups water

6-inch piece fresh ginger root, peeled and finely chopped

YAM CAKES:

12 tablespoons (1½ sticks) unsalted butter

1¼ cups granulated sugar

½ cup dark brown sugar

2 eggs

2 teaspoons vanilla extract

1½ cups cooked, peeled and mashed yams

2 cups cake flour

2 teaspoons baking powder

1½ tablespoons ground cinnamon

¼ teaspoon kosher or sea salt

¼ teaspoon ground cloves

¾ cup sultanas (golden raisins)

¾ cup coarsely chopped toasted walnuts or pecans

➤ These heavenly little nut- and raisin-studded cakes seem to have a divine effect on all who sample them. This is my favorite baked good; I never tire of their spicy-sweet flavor and moist texture.

HOT 1

makes 8 individual bundt cakes

To make the glaze: In a large, heavy-bottomed saucepan, combine the sugar, water, and ginger. Bring to a boil over moderate heat and cook 10 minutes, stirring occasionally and brushing the sides of the pan from time to time with a pastry brush dipped in cold water. Reduce the heat to moderately low and simmer 30 minutes without stirring, until thick and syrupy.

Remove from the heat and immediately strain through a fine wire mesh or sieve. Cool the syrup to room temperature. Cover with a tight-fitting lid and refrigerate for at least 2 hours before using. (May be refrigerated for up to 1 month.)

To make the Yam Cakes: Generously grease eight, 8-ounce capacity individual bundt pans or jumbo muffin tin cups; set aside. Preheat oven to 400° F.

In a large bowl, cream the butter until very soft. Add the sugars and beat until light and fluffy, about 5 minutes. Add the eggs and vanilla and beat well. Add the yams and mix thoroughly.

In a separate bowl, combine the flour, baking powder, cinnamon, salt, cloves, sultanas, and walnuts; mix thoroughly. Add to the wet ingredients and mix well. Spoon into prepared bundt pans and bake on lower shelf of oven 15 minutes. Reduce oven to 350° F. and rotate pans to upper shelf. Bake 15 to 20 minutes, or until a toothpick inserted into the center of a cake comes out clean. Remove from the oven and cool in pans 5 to 7 minutes. Gently remove cakes and cool on baking racks. When cool, brush with ginger glaze and serve immediately.

bittersweet chocolate ginger coins

To make crystallized ginger: In a 6-quart, heavy-bottomed saucepan, place the ginger and 2 quarts of cold water. Bring to a boil over high heat. Remove from heat and cool to room temperature. Drain well.

Return the ginger to the pan and add 2 quarts of fresh cold water. Add 2 cups of the granulated sugar and bring to a boil over moderate heat. Reduce heat and simmer 15 minutes. Cool to room temperature, cover, and let stand 8 hours or overnight.

Add 2 more cups of the granulated sugar and 1 cup of the corn syrup to the pan. Cover and bring to a boil over moderate heat; boil 5 minutes. Remove the cover and cook 20 minutes, stirring occasionally. Replace the cover, remove from the heat, and cool to room temperature. Let stand 8 hours or overnight.

Add the remaining 1 cup *each* granulated sugar and corn syrup; mix well. Bring to a boil over moderate heat. Boil 25 to 35 minutes, or until the ginger is tender and translucent. Remove from the heat, cover, and cool to room temperature. Using a slotted spoon, remove the ginger from the syrup and drain on baking racks overnight.

Place the 1½ cups castor or granulated sugar in a large bowl. Add the ginger and mix well using your fingers; take care to separate the ginger and coat each piece evenly with the sugar. Arrange the ginger in a single layer on a baking sheet.

To make the chocolate coins: Heat the chocolate in the top of a double boiler over moderately low heat until just melted. Using a spoon, drizzle the chocolate over the ginger to make fine stripes. When the chocolate is cool and firm, remove ginger and store in a tightly sealed box at room temperature for up to 1 month (several months without the chocolate).

➤ This recipe begins with directions for making crystallized ginger, which is then drizzled with bittersweet chocolate to make a sensational confection. Although you can purchase crystallized ginger ready-made, it's much more gratifying and fun to make it yourself. As a bonus, you end up with a super-concentrated ginger-flavored syrup you can add to iced beverages and hot tea, drizzle over ice cream or frozen yogurt, and use in all sorts of desserts. And once you see how easy the crystallizing process is, you'll be turning all kinds of fresh fruit into sugared jewels.

Be sure to use fat, round ginger roots with as few knobs as possible.

HOTTER 6

makes about 2½ cups ginger coins

12-inch section fresh ginger root, knobs removed, peeled and cut on the diagonal into ¼-inch-thick discs (about 2½ cups)

5 cups granulated sugar

2 cups corn syrup

1½ cups golden castor or granulated sugar, for coating

4 ounces bittersweet chocolate

frozen ginger-peach yogurt with cinnamon

2 cups vanilla low-fat yogurt

1 jar (7 ounces) marshmallow cream

3 large peaches, pitted and finely chopped

5-inch piece fresh ginger root, peeled and minced

1 tablespoon ground cinnamon

Fresh mint sprigs and/or ¼ cup finely chopped toasted almonds, for garnish

➤ You may never eat store-bought ice cream or frozen yogurt again after tasting the homemade version that follows. This summery, low-fat dessert can be frozen in a covered container in your freezer—you don't need an ice-cream maker for this treat.

HOTTER 4

makes about 6 servings

In a large bowl, whisk together 1 cup of the yogurt with the marshmallow cream until thoroughly combined. Add the remaining yogurt and mix until smooth. Add the peaches, ginger, and cinnamon and mix well. Transfer to a shallow, flat-bottomed plastic or stainless steel container and cover with a tight-fitting lid. Place in the freezer for 1 hour. Remove and stir vigorously with a fork. Return to the freezer and mix again in 2 hours. Return to the freezer and freeze until firm.

To present free-form in bowls, remove from the freezer 10 to 15 minutes prior to serving to soften slightly before spooning into small bowls. To serve in square or rectangular shapes on dessert plates, remove from the freezer and cut into the desired shapes. Serve immediately, garnished with mint sprigs and/or finely chopped toasted almonds.

mustard

◆　◆　◆　◆　◆　**MUSTARD**

Mustard lends itself particularly well to vegetarian fare. It provides a creamy richness to the palate yet contributes virtually no fat, adding pizzazz and depth to dishes that might otherwise be bland.

Because of these attributes, the dishes in this chapter are loaded with flavor and character, despite the absence of meat, poultry, fish, or seafood. I'd go so far as to say that even the most faithful meat-eater would enjoy these recipes.

This chapter includes an interesting variety of dishes, from such hors d'oeuvres and appetizers as *Triple-Mustard Mushroom Fritters* and *Chinese Vegetable Eggrolls with Mustard Sauce* to such tempting main courses as *Cabbage Rolls with Mustard-Spiked Vegetables* and *Rigatoni with Broccoli, Peppers, and Creamy Mustard Sauce.* There are no desserts, however; my sense of adventure in the kitchen has limits. But if you'd like to try a stripe of the stuff on your next éclair or a squiggle on a bowl of ice cream, be my guest.

The history of mustard dates back to the ancient Romans, who were the first to combine the seeds with vinegars, honey, spices, and nuts to form prepared mustard pastes. The name is thought to come from the Roman mixture of crushed mustard seeds and *must* (unfermented grape juice), which was called *mustum ardens,* or "burning wine."

A member of the *Cruciferae* family, mustard plants are annuals that produce bright yellow flowers and long, narrow, seed-filled pods. Black mustard, native to the Middle East and Asia, has been grown in Europe for centuries. Because this particular seed is difficult to harvest, however, it has not been widely cultivated for mass production. Brown mustard seed, originally from Asia, now grows throughout northern Europe and in parts of England. Less pungent than its black counterpart, this seed is favored by many mustard makers, who use it to produce full-flavored, pungent pastes. Native to the Mediterranean, yellow mustard seeds are now grown in eastern counties of England, in Canada, and in the United States. Less pungent than black or brown seeds, and larger than both, yellow seeds are used primarily in English and French, in some German, and in many American mustards; they are also ground and sold as mustard powder.

When purchasing whole mustard seeds, look for regular, even-colored, hard seeds. Store them in a tightly sealed jar or plastic bag in a cool, dark place for up to one year. Purchase mustard powder in individual sealed tins rather than in bulk, where it tends to lose its strength and intensity.

Prepared commercial mustards must be refrigerated once opened; properly stored, mustards are good for about four or five months, but kept longer they tend to lose their potency and flavor.

Like horseradish, fresh ginger, and many chili peppers, prepared mustard loses most of its punch when cooked for extended periods of time. When mustard seeds are crushed and mixed with cold or warm water, the enzyme myrosin mixes with the glucoside contained in the seeds, and forms a volatile oil characteristic of mustard. On the other hand, myrosin mixed with boiling water produces a bitter, unpleasant flavor, rendering the finished product undesirable. To avoid this and to yield the most pronounced flavor, add slightly crushed seeds or mustard paste at the end of cooking rather than at the beginning. To slightly crush mustard seeds, use an electric or manual spice grinder. Whole mustard seeds can be added at any time during the cooking process.

Prepared mustards act as a natural thickener, and since mustard is so low in calories and fat, it is a sensible and delicious thickening agent for many dishes. Commercially prepared mustards range from mild and smooth to sharp, biting, and coarse in texture. When cooking, intensely hot, pungent mustards naturally lend more flavor to cooked or heated dishes than do those with less emphatic properties. Although most mustards are exhilarating to the taste buds, some are truly fiery and sinus clearing.

The basic commercially prepared mustards called for in these recipes include tangy, bright-tasting yellow mustard (such as Gulden's yellow) and brown mustard, which has a mellower, deeper flavor than the yellow. Dijon mustard is excellent for cooking; its slightly sharp flavor blends well with many foods without being too subtle or too overpowering. German-style mustards sold commercially in this country range from mild, slightly sweet, yellow varieties to pungent, robustly flavored coarse-grained types. Bottled Chinese mustard is guaranteed to excite palates and blast sinuses; it should be used prudently as a condiment and in recipes.

If you enjoy preparing and eating dishes with pronounced, bold flavors, I suggest stocking at least five or six different styles of mustard. No kitchen is complete without the classic smooth Dijon, which is now available in coarse grind, too. Honey mustard, Chinese-style mustard, and one or two flavored varieties such as jalapeño or raspberry are also useful to have on hand. German-style coarse-ground and good old Gulden's mustard will round out your basic mustard pantry.

chinese vegetable eggrolls with mustard sauce

¹/₂ cup Chinese mustard powder, such as Oriental Hot Mustard

3 to 4 tablespoons cold water

1 tablespoon soy sauce

EGGROLLS:

1¹/₂ tablespoons peanut oil

3 stalks celery, trimmed, halved lengthwise, and thinly sliced

³/₄ cup finely chopped water chestnuts

1¹/₂ tablespoons brown mustard seeds

8 dried tree ear mushrooms (black fungus), reconstituted in warm water, drained, and finely chopped (about 1¹/₂ cups)

3 cloves garlic, finely chopped

5 cups finely shredded Napa cabbage

1¹/₂ tablespoons soy sauce

10 scallions, trimmed and finely chopped

(continued overleaf)

➤ Preparing homemade eggrolls is definitely a labor of love, but one well worth the effort. To break the preparation into stages, the filling may successfully be frozen separately; the uncooked but fully assembled eggrolls may also be frozen for up to one month.

The ingredients can be found at most full-service grocery stores, ethnic food markets, or Asian grocery stores.

HOT 3

makes about 20 eggrolls; 6 to 8 appetizer servings

To make the sauce: In a small bowl, combine the mustard powder, water, and soy sauce to form a smooth mixture for dipping. Set aside until needed.

To make the filling: In a very large wok or sauté pan, heat the peanut oil over high heat until it just begins to smoke. Add the celery, water chestnuts, and mustard seeds and cook, stirring constantly, 1¹/₂ minutes. Add the mushrooms and cook 30 seconds. Add the garlic, 3 cups of the cabbage, the soy sauce, scallions, and sugar; cook 1 to 1¹/₂ minutes, stirring constantly, until the cabbage is *just* wilted and the celery is crisp-tender.

Remove from the heat and transfer to a large bowl. Add the prepared mustard, black bean sauce, and remaining 2 cups cabbage. Season with salt and pepper and mix well. Cover tightly and refrigerate for at least 1¹/₂ hours, or up to 8 hours. (Filling also can be frozen in an airtight container for up to 1 month. Thaw and drain before assembling the eggrolls.)

To assemble the eggrolls: Combine the water and cornstarch to make a *slurry*. Place several egg roll skins on a flat surface. Brush the *slurry* approximately ¹/₂ inch around the edges of each skin. Place about 3 tablespoons of filling along the bottom edges closest to you, leaving about ¹/₂ inch of space at the sides. Fold the ¹/₂-inch sides in toward the center and over the filling at one end; press gently to seal. Beginning with the filled edge, roll each to form a tight cylinder. Assemble the remaining eggrolls in this fashion. Refrigerate until ready to cook. (At this point the eggrolls may also be tightly wrapped and frozen up to 1 month. Thaw in the refrigerator before cooking.)

(continued overleaf)

1 tablespoon sugar

1 tablespoon prepared hot
Chinese mustard

2 teaspoons Chinese hot
black bean sauce

Salt and pepper, to taste

1/3 cup cold water

3 tablespoons cornstarch

20 eggroll wrappers

3/4 to 1 cup vegetable oil,
for frying

To fry the eggrolls: In a 12-inch sauté pan, heat ½ cup of the vegetable oil over moderately high heat. When the oil is hot but not smoking, add 5 or 6 eggrolls. Cook, turning frequently to promote even browning, 1½ to 2 minutes, or until all sides are golden brown. Remove with tongs or a slotted spoon and drain on paper towels. Cook the remaining eggrolls in this fashion, adding more oil as needed. Serve immediately with the mustard dipping sauce.

east indian pickled mangoes with mustard seed

3 cups white vinegar

2 tablespoons coarsely
ground yellow mustard
seeds

1 tablespoon whole brown
mustard seeds

3 cloves garlic, thinly sliced

1/4 cup dark molasses

2 tablespoons kosher salt

2 large green mangoes
(about 1 1/2 pounds), halved,
pitted, and cut into 1/4-inch
wedges

➤ Serve this pungent condiment with a traditional East Indian feast or with grilled vegetables and steamed rice.

To allow time for the pickling process, prepare this condiment at least three weeks before you plan to serve it. Mangoes are usually available year-round, although the peak season in the United States is late spring through summer.

HOTTER 5

makes 10 to 12 servings

In a 4-quart saucepan, combine the vinegar, mustard, garlic, molasses, and salt. Bring to a boil over high heat and cook 15 minutes, stirring occasionally. Add the mango and cook 5 to 7 minutes, or until tender. Remove from the heat and cool to room temperature. Transfer to a nonreactive container with a tight-fitting lid and store in the refrigerator for at least 3 weeks before serving. Will keep in the refrigerator for up to 2 months.

root vegetable slaw with creamy mustard dressing

Place the beets in a small saucepan and cover with cold water. Bring to a boil over high heat, reduce the heat to moderate, cover, and cook 40 to 45 minutes, or until tender when pierced with a fork. Drain and cool to room temperature. Remove skins and cut into slivers. Set aside.

Blanch the carrots and celery root in a pot of boiling water. Drain well and refresh in cold water. Dry thoroughly and set aside.

In a large bowl, whisk together the olive oil, mustards, and honey to form a smooth mixture. Slowly add the vinegar and whisk to form a smooth emulsion. Add the coriander, parsley, and reserved carrots and celery root. Toss gently and season with salt and pepper. Just before serving, add the beets and walnuts; mix gently *just* until combined (avoid overmixing, lest the beets turn the entire mixture red). Serve on a bed of mustard greens.

➤ The contrasting flavors and colors of beets, carrots, and celery root combine to make a visually stunning, tasty, and healthful salad. Paired with rye crackers and Swiss cheese, this dish makes a fine autumn lunch.

HOTTEST 7

makes 4 to 6 servings

5 small beets, trimmed

3 carrots, slivered

2 small celery roots, trimmed, peeled, and slivered

1/2 cup olive oil

2 tablespoons prepared coarse-grained mustard

1 tablespoon prepared jalapeño or hot mustard

1 tablespoon honey

2 tablespoons apple cider vinegar

1 teaspoon ground coriander

1/4 cup finely chopped fresh parsley

Salt and pepper, to taste

1/3 cup coarsely chopped toasted walnuts

Mustard greens, for lining platter

english cheddar cheese soup with brown mustard and ale

4 tablespoons unsalted butter

4 tablespoons all-purpose flour

1 tablespoon brown mustard seeds

1 teaspoon ground caraway seeds

1/4 cup prepared brown or German-style mustard

2 cups dark ale

6 cups homemade vegetable stock (page 13) or canned vegetable broth (preferably low-sodium)

2 cups whole milk

1 pound sharp English Cheddar cheese, coarsely grated

Salt and pepper, to taste

➤ This hearty soup is satisfying and filling, especially when paired with a pint of ale and dark bread spread with sweet butter.

HOT 2

makes about 6 servings

In a heavy-bottomed, 6-quart pot, melt the butter over moderate heat. Add the flour, mix to form a paste, and cook over moderately low heat 5 to 7 minutes, stirring frequently, until light golden brown. Add the mustard seeds, caraway seeds, and prepared mustard and cook 2 minutes, stirring constantly.

Slowly add the ale, whisking constantly with a wire whisk to form a smooth mixture. Add the vegetable stock and milk and bring to a boil over high heat, whisking constantly to prevent lumps from forming. Boil for 25 to 30 minutes, stirring occasionally, until the mixture is slightly thick and no lumps remain. (If there are any lumps at this point, strain through a fine wire mesh or sieve and return to the pan.)

Add the cheese, stirring constantly until thoroughly melted, about 3 minutes. Remove from the heat, season with salt and pepper, and serve immediately.

braised winter vegetables with lemon-mustard sauce

In a large pot, bring 1 quart of salted water to boil over high heat. Add the onions and return to the boil. Reduce the heat to moderately high and cook 9 or 10 minutes, or until they are tender but not mushy. Drain immediately and cool to room temperature. When cool enough to handle, remove the skins and trim root ends. Set aside until needed.

In a shallow-sided skillet, cook the carrots, turnips, and mustard seeds in the olive oil and butter over moderate heat 10 minutes, stirring occasionally. Add the reserved onions, vegetable stock, prepared mustard, lemon juice, and lemon zest and mix well. Cook 3 to 4 minutes, stirring frequently, until the vegetables are coated with the sauce. Season with salt and pepper and serve immediately, garnished with minced parsley.

➤ Although this vegetable dish looks and tastes rich and creamy, the piquant sauce is made with only one tablespoon of butter—and no cream.

HOT 1

makes 4 to 6 servings

8 small pearl onions, trimmed and peeled

3 carrots, trimmed and cut on the diagonal into ³/₄-inch-long pieces

2 turnips, trimmed, quartered, and cut into ³/₄-inch wedges

1 tablespoon yellow mustard seeds

2 tablespoons olive oil

1 tablespoon unsalted butter

¹/₂ cup homemade vegetable stock (page 13) or canned vegetable broth (preferably low-sodium)

¹/₄ cup prepared champagne or Dijon mustard

2 tablespoons fresh lemon juice

Grated zest from 1 lemon

Salt and pepper, to taste

¹/₄ cup minced fresh parsley, for garnish (optional)

baked mustard-molasses black-eyed peas

1 large onion, cut into small dice

3 cloves garlic, minced

1½ tablespoons peanut or vegetable oil

3 cups cooked black-eyed peas

⅔ cup prepared Gulden's or other yellow mustard

¼ cup dark molasses

2½ tablespoons unsalted butter, cut into small pieces

2 tablespoons mustard powder

2½ tablespoons red wine vinegar

Salt and pepper, to taste

➤ Present this rustic American-style dish for supper on a wintery evening with a green salad of mild and bitter greens and black bread and butter. Mugs of Oktoberfest beer would top it off perfectly.

HOT 2

makes 4 to 6 servings

Preheat oven to 375° F.

In a large sauté pan, cook the onion and garlic in the oil over moderate heat 7 or 8 minutes, or until light golden brown. Transfer to a 1½-quart ovenproof casserole. Add the cooked black-eyed peas, prepared mustard, molasses, butter, mustard powder, and red wine vinegar. Mix well and season with salt and pepper. Cover with foil and bake in the center of the oven 30 minutes. Remove foil and bake on upper shelf of oven 10 to 15 minutes, or until edges and top are bubbling and toasty brown. Serve immediately.

mustard-glazed wild mushroom ragoût

3/4 pound portobello mushrooms, stemmed and cut into 1/2-inch pieces

3/4 pound domestic brown or button mushrooms, stemmed and quartered

3 tablespoons olive oil

1 tablespoon unsalted butter

3 shallots, thinly sliced

3 cloves garlic, minced

1 1/2 teaspoons dried thyme

1 teaspoon rubbed sage

1/3 pound shiitake mushrooms, stemmed and cut into 1/2-inch pieces

1/4 pound medium oyster mushrooms, halved

1/3 cup dry sherry

1/4 cup mushroom soy sauce

1/4 cup prepared Dijon mustard

2 tablespoons prepared champagne mustard or other mild mustard

3 tablespoons half-and-half

Salt and pepper, to taste

1/4 cup minced fresh parsley, for garnish

➤ This elegant mushroom dish goes together quickly and easily. It makes an outstanding companion to grilled polenta, mixed white and wild rices, mashed potatoes, or cooked pasta.

HOT 1

makes 4 to 6 servings

In a large, nonstick sauté pan, cook the portobello and brown mushrooms in 2 tablespoons of the olive oil over moderately high heat, stirring occasionally, until any liquid has evaporated and the mushrooms are very light golden brown. Remove from the pan and transfer to a bowl. Set aside.

In the same pan, heat the remaining tablespoon of olive oil and the butter. Add the shallots, garlic, herbs, and shiitake and oyster mushrooms and cook over moderate heat, stirring occasionally, until shallots and mushrooms are tender. Add the reserved mushrooms, the sherry, soy sauce, mustards, and half-and-half. Mix gently and cook 6 or 7 minutes, stirring occasionally, until mixture is slightly thick and aromatic.

Season with salt and pepper, garnish with parsley, and serve immediately.

triple-mustard mushroom fritters

In a large bowl, combine the flour, mustard powder, baking powder, and mustard seeds; mix well and set aside.

In a small bowl, whisk together the butter, egg yolks (refrigerate the whites until ready to use), garlic, Dijon mustard, sage, salt, and pepper. Slowly add the milk, whisking constantly to form a smooth emulsion. Add to the dry ingredients, whisking constantly to form a smooth mixture. (You may switch to a wooden spoon once the two components are thoroughly combined.)

Cover with plastic and refrigerate for at least 4 hours or overnight.

Just before cooking, beat the egg whites until stiff but not dry. Fold the whites into the batter and stir gently until *just* mixed.

In a large, heavy-bottomed saucepan, heat 4 inches of oil over moderately high heat until hot but not smoking. Select as many mushrooms as will comfortably fit in one layer in the oil-filled saucepan, and drop them into the batter. Make sure each mushroom is completely covered with the batter as you remove them with a slotted spoon or tongs. Drop immediately into the hot oil and cook, turning as needed, until well browned on all sides and slightly puffy. Remove with a slotted spoon and drain on paper towels. Let the oil come back up to the proper temperature before adding another batch of mushrooms. Cook the remaining mushrooms in this fashion, adding more oil as needed. Serve immediately, garnished with lemon wedges.

➤ Don't let the long ingredient list or seemingly complicated instructions frighten you away. The fritters are quite simple to prepare and cook, and the results are sensational. They make an outstanding hors d'oeuvre for cocktail parties or a formal dinner.

HOT 2

makes about 6 servings

1 1/4 cups all-purpose flour

2 tablespoons mustard powder

1/2 teaspoon baking powder

1 1/2 tablespoons yellow mustard seeds

3 tablespoons unsalted butter, melted and cooled to room temperature

2 eggs, separated

2 cloves garlic, minced

2 tablespoons prepared Dijon mustard

1 teaspoon rubbed sage

1 teaspoon kosher salt

1/2 teaspoon black pepper

1 cup whole milk

3 to 4 cups vegetable oil, for cooking

1 pound small button mushrooms, wiped clean and trimmed

Lemon wedges, for garnish

cabbage rolls with mustard-spiked vegetables

To prepare the cabbage leaves: Fill with salted water a pot large enough to accommodate the entire head of cabbage. Bring to a boil over high heat. Drop the head of cabbage in the boiling water for about 1 minute, or until the outer leaves are soft and pliable. Remove the entire head from the water, and gently remove as many of the outer leaves as possible without tearing them. Return the head to the water and repeat the process until you have 12 to 15 whole leaves without any tears. At the bottom of each leaf, cut a 'V' shape to remove the tough, fibrous vein.

If the leaves are not pliable enough to mold around the filling and form into rolls, drop individually into the boiling water and cook 20 to 30 seconds or until pliable but not overcooked and too soft. Drain between layers of paper towels. Set aside until needed.

To make the filling: In a very large sauté pan, cook the onion, garlic, mustard seeds, and spices in the *ghee* over high heat 3 minutes, stirring frequently, until the spices are aromatic. Add the water and cook 3 minutes, stirring frequently. Add the carrot, tomatoes, and chickpeas and bring to a boil. Reduce the heat to moderately low and cook, stirring occasionally, 35 to 40 minutes, or until all the vegetables are tender and the mixture is thick. Remove from the heat and cool slightly. Add the prepared mustard and season with salt and pepper; mix well.

To make the cabbage rolls: Preheat oven to 400° F. Lightly grease a 9-x-12-inch baking pan. Place the cabbage leaves on a flat surface, with the V-shaped cuts closest to you. Close the triangle by bringing the cut corners of the cabbage leaf together to form an unbroken circle. Along the bottom of the leaf, place 2 to 3 tablespoons of the filling.

(continued overleaf)

➤ The filling for these zesty cabbage rolls may be made one or two days in advance and refrigerated until ready to use.

Loaded with nutrition and packed with flavor, these rolls are terrific served with a smooth tomato sauce or drizzled with plain yogurt.

HOT 2

makes about 12 rolls; 6 servings

1 **very large head white cabbage, cored**

1 **large onion, finely chopped**

3 **cloves garlic, finely chopped**

2 **tablespoons brown mustard seeds**

1 **tablespoon ground cumin**

2 **teaspoons** *each* **ground coriander, fenugreek, fennel seeds, and turmeric**

½ **teaspoon** *each* **ground cloves and caraway seeds**

3 **tablespoons** *ghee* **or vegetable oil (see note, p. 53)**

½ **cup water**

1 **small carrot, finely diced**

2 **cups peeled, seeded, and finely chopped tomatoes**

1½ **cups cooked chickpeas, coarsely chopped, plus** 1 **cup whole cooked chickpeas**

3 **tablespoons prepared brown mustard**

Salt and pepper, to taste

Begin rolling, folding the sides of the leaf in over the filling as you go, forming a neat, tight roll. Assemble the remaining leaves and filling in this fashion, taking care to completely enclose the filling within the leaves. Place in the prepared pan, cover tightly with tinfoil, and bake 10 to 12 minutes, or until the rolls are heated through. Serve immediately with additional mustard on the side, if desired.

mustard-glazed pumpkin wedges

1 tablespoon softened unsalted butter, cut into 4 pieces

1/3 cup dry sherry

1/4 cup Dijon mustard

1/4 cup whole milk

3 1/2 tablespoons brown mustard seeds

2 teaspoons ground coriander

2 tablespoons peanut oil

1 small eating pumpkin (about 1 pound), peeled, seeded, and cut into 1/2-inch-thick wedges (18 to 20 wedges)

Splash sherry vinegar or apple cider vinegar

Salt and pepper, to taste

➤ Serve this savory vegetable side dish with a salad of mixed baby greens tossed with pears and garnished with toasted walnuts and blue cheese. Warm rolls and butter, or even a basket of interesting crackers, would complete the meal.

HOT 1

makes about 6 servings

In a small bowl, combine the butter, sherry, Dijon mustard, milk, mustard seeds, and coriander. Mix until well combined; set aside.

In a very large, nonstick sauté pan, heat the peanut oil over moderate heat until warm. Add the pumpkin wedges and cook, stirring frequently, 5 to 7 minutes, or until light golden brown on all sides. Add the sherry-mustard mixture and cook 4 or 5 minutes, stirring gently, until the pumpkin is tender and the sauce is thick and aromatic. Add the vinegar and season with salt and pepper. Serve immediately.

rigatoni with broccoli, peppers, and creamy mustard sauce

5 cloves garlic, finely chopped

1 ½ tablespoons olive oil

3 cups heavy cream

1 teaspoon dried thyme

1 large red bell pepper, cut into ¾-inch-long rectangles or triangles

3 tablespoons prepared Dijon mustard

3 tablespoons prepared coarse-grained mustard

1 pound rigatoni pasta

3 cups broccoli flowerettes

1 cup toasted walnuts, coarsely chopped

Salt and pepper, to taste

➤ This luscious, cream-based pasta dish is a comforting indulgence that will satisfy cravings for something special. Accompany with a crisp sauvignon blanc or chenin blanc and warm, crusty bread.

HOT 2

makes about 6 servings

In a 12-quart pot, bring 8 quarts salted water to a boil over high heat.

Meanwhile, in a large sauté pan, cook the garlic in the olive oil over moderately low heat 5 minutes, or until very light golden brown. Add the cream and thyme and cook about 15 minutes, stirring frequently to prevent the mixture from boiling over. Add the bell pepper and mustards; mix well and remove from the heat.

Add the rigatoni to the boiling water, return to the boil, and stir well. Cook over high heat 12 minutes, or until pasta is *al dente*. Add the broccoli flowerettes and cook 20 seconds longer. Immediately drain in a colander and shake until no water remains. Place in a very large, preheated bowl and cover with a kitchen towel.

Reheat the cream mixture over high heat 2 to 3 minutes, stirring constantly, until the mixture is hot and bubbling and the pepper is crisp-tender. Immediately add to the pasta and broccoli, along with the walnuts, and toss gently. Season with salt and pepper and serve immediately.

note: to make ghee

In a small saucepan, heat 1 cup of clarified butter over moderately low heat until nearly simmering. Remove from the heat and let stand at room temperature for a few minutes. Pour into a glass container, and let stand until sediment falls to the bottom. Carefully pour the clear portion into a clean saucepan, leaving the sediment. Follow the same procedure one or two more times, or until no sediment remains. Pour through four layers of cheesecloth into a clean container. Cool to room temperature. Cover tightly and store in the refrigerator for up to 4 months. Makes about ½ cup.

peppercorns

The little black peppercorns we so took for granted have finally earned a spot on the shelves of gourmet food shops. Not just one, but five or six different varieties are now available in most specialty food shops. Although they cost only pennies per pound, black, white, pink, and green peppercorns now share the limelight with such glamorous and pricey seasonings as saffron and vanilla.

It takes a lot of pepper to make a dish truly blazing, but achieving that point often means obliterating other flavors to the extent that only one taste dominates—pepper. That isn't the goal with these recipes; on the contrary, the dishes presented here highlight the subtle flavor nuances among the peppercorn varieties.

Although all peppercorns provide plenty of heat, they each lend a distinct taste to a dish. For example, when comparing the three black varieties, Tellicherry, Lampong, and Malaba, I find each one to have a unique character. Tellicherry, one of the types most commonly found in retail shops, is at once fruity, spicy, and hot. Lampong is also fruity, but rounded rather than sharp in flavor, and mild in comparison. Malaba has a sharp, pointed flavor with a hot, fiery focus.

The variations among the peppercorn types—pink, green, black, and white—provide an interesting study for the culinary student and a challenge to the detail-oriented cook. But for regular folks and plain old hotheads, freshly ground whole black peppercorns are all that's needed to turn a bland, uneventful dish into something tasty and stimulating.

Traditionally used solely for savory dishes, black, white, and pink peppercorns also are beginning to appear in baked goods and other confections; I particularly like pairing black pepper with semisweet chocolate and even white chocolate. It also marries well with such dried fruits as prunes, figs, and dates, as well as such fresh fruits as melon, berries, plums, pears, and figs.

I urge you to try the three unique and striking desserts included here. Hotheads probably need no encouragement, but if the thought of combining sweets with peppercorns is too foreign, try using just half the amount of pepper suggested in each dessert recipe and see how you like the effect.

Native to Indonesia and the tropical forest and equatorial regions of India, pepper is still cultivated in Indonesia and India as well as Malaysia, Brazil, the West Indies, eastern Asia, Cambodia, and Madagascar. *Piper nigrum,* a species of *Piper,* is a climbing plant with 3- to 7-inch heart-shaped green leaves and flowers that bear clustered fruit. Depending on the level of maturity and how they are treated once picked, these fruits eventually come to market as either black, white, or green peppercorns.

When purchasing dried peppercorns, look for whole peppercorns sold in bulk or packed in tightly sealed tubes or containers. To check the freshness, rub a few peppercorns between your fingers and sniff for a pronounced aroma. Black and white pepper are sold preground, but avoid purchasing pepper in this form. Preground pepper often includes fillers and other unwanted ingredients and is usually stale.

I recommend grinding dry peppercorns in a spice or coffee mill for cooking purposes. For the table I prefer an adjustable pepper mill so that the peppercorns can be ground fine, medium, or coarse. A mortar and pestle is convenient for extremely coarse grinding and bruising.

To bruise peppercorns in a mortar and pestle, place the spice in the center of the mortar and lightly rub with the pestle until the desired texture is achieved. To bruise or grind without a pepper mill, mortar and pestle, or electric grinder, place the spice in a medium-sized bowl and use a smaller bowl that fits inside it to rub and crush the peppercorns. You also can place the peppercorns on a cutting board and press gently with a heavy skillet or rolling pin until they are bruised. If you try to bruise or crush the peppercorns too aggressively at first they will fly all over the room. Be gentle until they are bruised and then, if desired, you can use more force to grind them smaller.

BLACK PEPPERCORNS, PICKED BEFORE THEY FULLY RIPEN, ARE DRIED IN THE SUN FOR EIGHT TO TEN DAYS UNTIL THEY SHRINK AND SHRIVEL AND ARE HARD, DRY, AND BLACK. THERE ARE MANY VARIETIES OF BLACK PEPPER, EACH WITH A DISTINCTIVE TASTE AND AROMA. MOST POPULAR ARE TELLICHERRY AND LAMPONG PEPPERCORNS, BUT WELL-STOCKED SPECIALTY OR SPICE SHOPS OFTEN CARRY SINGAPORE, PENANG, MALABA, AND ALLEPPEY VARIETIES AS WELL.

·····

WHITE PEPPERCORNS ARE PICKED RIPE AND THEN TREATED TO A WATER BATH IN ORDER TO REMOVE THE OUTER SKINS. ONCE THE SKIN IS RUBBED OFF, THE INNER PORTION IS DRIED UNTIL IT TURNS A PALE SHADE OF OFF-WHITE. IN COMPARISON TO THE BLACK PEPPERCORN, THE WHITE VARIETY IS SMALLER AND SOFTER, CONTAINS A HIGHER PERCENTAGE OF PIPERINE (A HEAT-LENDING ALKALOID), BUT HAS FEWER AROMATIC ELEMENTS, THUS RENDERING IT MORE FIERY BUT LESS FLAVORFUL. THE MOST COMMON TYPES AVAILABLE INCLUDE MUNTOK, SARAWAK, AND SIAM.

·····

GREEN PEPPERCORNS ARE PICKED UNRIPE, BUT UNLIKE THOSE PROCESSED TO MAKE BLACK PEPPERCORNS, THEY ARE IMMEDIATELY FREEZE-DRIED OR PRESERVED IN BRINE. LESS PUNGENT THAN BLACK OR WHITE PEPPERCORNS, FRUITY-TASTING GREEN PEPPERCORNS ARE TRADITIONALLY PAIRED WITH SUCH MILDER-TASTING MEATS AS CHICKEN, PORK, AND VEAL AND WITH FISH AND SEAFOOD. WHILE TRAVELING IN THAILAND, I SAMPLED SEVERAL DISHES THAT INCLUDED SMALL BUNCHES OF FRESH GREEN PEPPERCORNS ON THE STEM—THEY WERE EXTREMELY PUNGENT!

·····

PINK PEPPERCORNS, TECHNICALLY SPEAKING, ARE NOT CONSIDERED TRUE PEPPER BUT RATHER THE DRIED BERRIES FROM A SOUTH AMERICAN TREE. ACCORDING TO SOME REFERENCES, THIS UNDERAPPRECIATED SPICE IS DERIVED FROM *SHINUS TEREBINTHIFOLIUS*; OTHERS LIST THE SOURCE AS *SHINUS MOLLE*. IN ANY EVENT, PINK PEPPERCORNS ARE USUALLY FREEZE-DRIED OR PACKED IN BRINE AND CAN BE FOUND IN SPECIALTY FOOD STORES OR SPICE SHOPS. USE THESE AROMATIC, SLIGHTLY SWEET, DISTINCTIVE, AND PUNGENT PEPPERCORNS IN CREAM OR BUTTER SAUCES; WITH POULTRY, FISH, AND SEAFOOD; AND IN DESSERTS THAT BEG FOR A FLOWERY, SPICY FLAVOR FOLLOWED BY A HINT OF WARMTH.

·····

peppery cheddar cheese crisps

1 1/4 cups all-purpose flour

1/2 cup fine yellow cornmeal

1/2 teaspoon baking powder

2 tablespoons black peppercorns, coarsely ground

1 teaspoon kosher or sea
salt

10 tablespoons (1 1/4 sticks)
unsalted butter, cut into
small pieces

1/2 pound sharp Cheddar
cheese, finely grated

3 to 3 1/2 tablespoons
seltzer water

➤ Judging from the speed
and enthusiasm with which
they are gobbled up every time
I make them, I suggest hiding
these habit-forming crackers
until you're ready to serve them.
They're great with a crisp white
wine or pale ale.

HOT 3

makes 55 to 60 crackers

Combine the flour, cornmeal, baking powder, black pepper, and salt in a medium bowl; mix well. Add the butter and cheese and, using your fingers, quickly mix them into the dry ingredients until a well-blended dough forms. Add just enough water to form a smooth, pliable dough. Gather into a ball and place on a cutting board.

Divide the ball into four equal pieces and shape each into a ball. Press and roll each into a long cylinder, approximately 1 1/4 inches in diameter. Wrap each cylinder in plastic wrap and refrigerate at least 4 hours or up to 2 days.

Preheat oven to 400° F. Remove the dough from the refrigerator. Using a very sharp knife, cut the dough into 1/8-inch-thick (or thinner, if possible) rounds. (You may want to run the knife under very hot water from time to time to facilitate cutting the dough.) Arrange the rounds on *ungreased* baking sheets, leaving approximately a 3/4-inch space between each one. Bake 7 or 8 minutes until light golden brown, rotating the pans once to encourage even baking. Using a spatula, immediately remove from baking sheets to wire cooling racks. When cool, store in tightly sealed plastic bags or an airtight container at room temperature for up to 4 days.

chilled cream of asparagus soup with green peppercorns

1 1/2 pounds asparagus, trimmed, stalks coarsely chopped, and tips reserved

3 shallots, coarsely chopped

1 1/2 tablespoons green peppercorns, finely ground

2 tablespoons vegetable or light olive oil

5 cups homemade vegetable stock (page 13) or canned vegetable broth (preferably low-sodium)

1 1/2 cups whipping cream

Salt and pepper, to taste

1/3 cup finely chopped fresh chives, for garnish (optional)

➤ Pair this silky soup with a salad of mixed greens for a delightful spring or summer lunch. Combined with a composed salad of assorted spring vegetables and warm rolls, the soup becomes a complete dinner.

HOT 2

makes 4 to 6 servings

In a 3-quart, heavy-bottomed saucepan, sauté the asparagus stalks (not the tips), shallots, and peppercorns in the vegetable oil over moderately high heat 3 to 5 minutes, stirring occasionally. Add the vegetable stock and cream and bring to a boil over high heat, stirring frequently to prevent the mixture from boiling over. Reduce the heat to moderate and cook 8 to 10 minutes, or until asparagus is tender but not mushy. Remove from the heat and cool slightly.

Using a blender, purée the mixture in batches until smooth. Strain through a fine wire mesh or sieve and return to the saucepan. Bring to a boil over high heat, stirring frequently. Add the reserved asparagus tips and cook 1 minute, or until bright green and crisp-tender. Season with salt and pepper and remove from the heat.

Store in a tightly sealed container in the refrigerator until thoroughly chilled, about 4 hours. Serve cold, garnished with the chives, if desired.

sherried pumpkin bisque with pink and green peppercorns

In a heavy-bottomed, 12-quart pot, cook the onion in the olive oil and butter over moderate heat 5 minutes. Add the green peppercorns, coriander, allspice, mace, cloves, and pumpkin and cook, stirring constantly, 7 minutes. Add the vegetable stock and cream and bring to a boil over high heat. Reduce the heat to moderate and simmer 20 minutes or until the pumpkin is very tender. Cool slightly.

In a blender, purée the mixture in batches until very smooth. Return to the pot and add the sherry, vinegar, and pink peppercorns. Bring to a boil over high heat, stirring frequently. Reduce the heat to moderate and cook 10 minutes. Season with salt and pepper. Serve immediately.

➤ When crisp, cool days bring cravings for a heartwarming and soothing vegetable soup, serve this velvety bisque. Its spicy, rich flavors will brighten even the dreariest day.

HOTTER 4

makes about 6 servings

1 large onion, coarsely chopped

2 tablespoons olive oil

2 tablespoons unsalted butter

2 tablespoons green peppercorns

1 tablespoon ground coriander

1/2 teaspoon *each* ground allspice and mace

1/4 teaspoon ground cloves

1 small eating pumpkin (about 3 pounds), stemmed, halved, peeled, seeded, and cut into small dice (about 6 cups diced)

8 cups homemade vegetable stock (page 13) or canned vegetable broth (preferably low-sodium)

2 cups whipping cream

1 cup dry sherry

1 1/2 tablespoons sherry vinegar

2 1/2 tablespoons pink peppercorns

Salt and pepper, to taste

two-peppercorn broccoli timbales

Preheat oven to 325° F. Lightly grease a six-cup jumbo muffin tin.

In a large bowl, beat the eggs until well mixed. Add the cream, cheeses, peppercorns, thyme, salt, nutmeg, and broccoli; mix well. Evenly distribute the broccoli and peppercorns among the six muffin cups. Pour the egg mixture over the broccoli.

Set the muffin tin in a 9-x-13-inch baking pan. Fill the baking pan with very hot water until it reaches just over halfway up the sides of the muffin tin. Bake in the center of the oven 45 to 50 minutes, or until a toothpick inserted into the centers comes out clean. Remove from the oven and let stand at room temperature for 10 minutes before unmolding.

To unmold: Hold a baking sheet tightly over the muffin pan. With one quick motion, flip both pans over together, so that the timbales gently fall onto the baking sheet. Place the baking sheet on a flat surface and gently lift the muffin pan. Arrange on plates and serve immediately.

➤ For the consummate special-occasion meal, present these individual vegetable custards surrounded by angel hair pasta that has been anointed with good olive oil and laced with fresh herbs.

I use a jumbo muffin pan composed of six ²/₃-cup capacity muffin cups for this elegant dish.

HOT 3

makes 4 servings

4 eggs

2 cups heavy cream, warmed

2 ounces Parmesan cheese, finely grated

2 ounces Monterey Jack cheese, finely grated

1 ¹/₂ tablespoons coarsely ground white peppercorns

1 ¹/₂ tablespoons pink peppercorns

2 teaspoons dried thyme

1 teaspoon kosher or sea salt

¹/₂ teaspoon ground nutmeg

3 ¹/₂ cups small broccoli flowerettes, blanched

peppered summer squash frittata

3 small zucchini, cut into
¼-inch cubes

2 small yellow crookneck
squash, cut into ¼-inch
cubes

2 small pattypan squash, cut
into ¼-inch cubes

1 small onion, finely diced

2 tablespoons peanut or
vegetable oil

12 large eggs

2 teaspoons *each* white and
black peppercorns, coarsely
ground

1 teaspoon pink peppercorns

1½ tablespoons minced
fresh thyme

Fresh herb sprigs, for garnish

➤ Simple to make and easy to transport, this versatile summer-vegetable frittata is a great do-ahead dish for everything from small get-togethers to large picnics. Accompany with imported olives, assorted cheeses, and crackers and bread.

The recipe can easily be doubled and baked in two 10-inch sauté pans.

HOTTER 4

makes about 6 servings

Preheat oven to 325° F.

In a large sauté pan, cook the squash and onion in the oil over high heat, stirring frequently, 3 to 4 minutes or until crisp-tender. Transfer to a large bowl and cool to room temperature. When cool, add the eggs, peppercorns, and thyme. Mix well.

Place a nonstick ovenproof 10-inch sauté pan (with sloped sides) over moderately high heat. When the pan is warm, add the egg mixture and stir quickly from the outside of the pan toward the center (as if making scrambled eggs), until about one quarter of the mixture is set. Smooth the top, remove from the heat, and transfer to the middle rack of the oven. Bake 25 to 30 minutes, or until the center is set. Do not overbake the frittata. Remove from the oven and cool to room temperature.

To unmold, run a dull knife around the outside edges of the pan, gently pulling the frittata up and toward the center to loosen it from the bottom of the pan. Firmly hold a platter over the top of the pan and, with one quick movement, flip the pan and the platter over together, so that the frittata gently unmolds onto the platter. Serve at room temperature, sliced into wedges and garnished with herb sprigs.

winter root vegetable gratin with peppercorns

Preheat oven to 400° F. Generously grease a 9-x-12-inch baking pan.

In a very large bowl, combine the cream, peppercorns, nutmeg, and orange zest. Set aside.

Bring 4 quarts of salted water to boil in a large pot. Add the parsnips, turnips, and rutabaga and cook 2 minutes. Drain immediately in a colander and add to the cream; toss gently. Transfer to the prepared pan and place on the middle rack of the oven. Bake 30 minutes. Remove from the oven and evenly sprinkle the bread crumbs over the top. Return to the oven and bake 25 to 30 minutes, or until the top is brown and the vegetables are tender. Remove from the oven and let stand at room temperature 5 to 7 minutes before cutting into squares or rectangles. Garnish with the parsley.

➤ In cool-weather months, nothing satisfies like these earthy root vegetables cloaked in a rich, peppercorn-accented cream sauce. For a substantial lunch or light supper, pair with a salad of mixed greens tossed with apples and garnished with toasted walnuts.

HOT 2

makes 6 to 8 servings

3 1/2 cups whipping cream

1 tablespoon finely ground black peppercorns

1 1/2 teaspoons coarsely ground white peppercorns

1 teaspoon finely ground green peppercorns

1/2 teaspoon ground nutmeg

1 tablespoon finely minced orange zest

4 medium parsnips, trimmed and thinly sliced on the diagonal

2 small turnips, trimmed, halved, and thinly sliced

1 medium rutabaga, trimmed, halved, and thinly sliced

1 cup finely ground dried bread crumbs

1/3 cup minced fresh parsley, for garnish

three-pepper corn muffins

1 1/2 cups fine yellow cornmeal

1 cup unbleached or all-purpose flour

1/2 cup sugar

1 tablespoon *each* black and white peppercorns, coarsely ground

2 teaspoons green peppercorns

1 teaspoon kosher salt

1 1/4 cups buttermilk

3 large eggs

12 tablespoons (1 1/2 sticks) unsalted butter, melted and cooled slightly

1/3 pound sharp Cheddar cheese, finely grated

➤ Even my mom, who isn't a fan of corn bread, found these plump corn muffins, enriched with Cheddar cheese and spiked with peppercorns, tempting and delicious.

Serve with red beans and rice, black-eyed peas, or meatless Louisiana-style gumbo. These muffins are also good spread with softened cream cheese and topped with fresh tomato slices.

HOT 3

makes 12 standard muffins or 6 jumbo muffins

Preheat oven to 350° F. Generously grease two standard muffin tins (12 cups) or one jumbo muffin tin (6 cups).

In a large bowl, combine the cornmeal, flour, sugar, peppercorns, and salt. Mix well and set aside.

In a medium bowl, combine the buttermilk and eggs, whisking well to thoroughly combine. Add the butter and cheese and mix well.

Make a well in the center of the dry ingredients. Slowly add the wet ingredients, mixing with a large fork until *just combined*. Do not overmix the batter. Using a large spoon, fill each muffin cup three-quarters full with batter. Place the pan(s) on the bottom rack of the oven and bake 10 minutes, rotating the pan(s) once from front to back. Place pan(s) on top rack and bake an additional 7 or 8 minutes, or until a toothpick inserted in the center of a muffin comes out clean and the tops are barely light golden brown. Do not overbake the muffins.

Remove from the oven and let stand 5 to 7 minutes. Gently remove muffins from pans and cool on racks. Serve warm or at room temperature. Muffins may be stored tightly wrapped in foil at room temperature for 1 or 2 days.

dark chocolate bread pudding with black pepper

Preheat oven to 300° F. Place the bread cubes on a large baking sheet in a single layer. Toast 7 to 10 minutes or until crisp and very light brown on all sides. Remove from oven and cool to room temperature. Set aside.

In a 4-quart heavy-bottomed saucepan, combine the half-and-half, milk, and semisweet chocolate. Heat over moderately low heat for 3 to 4 minutes, stirring frequently, until the chocolate has completely melted. Mix well, remove from the heat, and cool slightly.

In a large bowl, whisk together the eggs, sugar, whiskey, vanilla extract, and salt. Add the cooled chocolate-cream mixture and mix well. Add the pepper, cinnamon, and reserved bread cubes; toss gently. Let stand at room temperature for 1 to 1½ hours, pressing the bread down into the liquid every 20 minutes to promote even saturation. Add the bittersweet chocolate and walnuts and toss gently.

Preheat oven to 350° F. Generously grease a shallow 3-quart ovenproof casserole.

Turn the bread mixture into the prepared casserole and bake on the middle rack of the oven 15 minutes. Reduce oven temperature to 325° F. and bake 25 to 30 minutes, or until the center jiggles slightly when shaken. Remove from the oven and let stand 5 to 10 minutes before serving.

> Bread pudding will have new appeal once you sample this unique and delectable rendition. Although it's pleasing as is, you may gild the lily by drizzling the warm pudding with crème fraîche or vanilla yogurt, or by garnishing it with dollops of whipped cream or coffee ice cream.

HOT 2
makes 6 to 8 servings

1 baguette (8 ounces), halved lengthwise and cut into 1-inch cubes (about 5 cups cubed)

1½ cups half-and-half

1½ cups whole milk

4 ounces semisweet chocolate, coarsely chopped

3 large eggs

²/₃ cup sugar

¼ cup whiskey or rum

1½ teaspoons vanilla extract

Dash kosher salt

1½ tablespoons black peppercorns, very coarsely ground

1½ teaspoons ground cinnamon

4 ounces bittersweet chocolate, very coarsely chopped

³/₄ cup walnuts, very coarsely chopped

frozen white chocolate mousse with black pepper

2 cups whipping cream

12 ounces white chocolate, coarsely chopped

1 jar (7 ounces) marshmallow cream

1 1/2 tablespoons crème de cacao

2 teaspoons vanilla extract

2 teaspoons very coarsely ground black peppercorns

Mint sprigs, for garnish

➤ You may serve this decadent dessert in a pool of fresh berry or dark chocolate sauce; with sliced fresh fruit; or simply garnished with fresh mint.

Instead of making an elaborate stove-top Italian-style meringue as called for in many mousse recipes, this easy-to-make dessert uses convenient jarred marshmallow cream—a terrific and versatile commercial product.

HOT 3

makes 6 to 8 servings

Place 1 1/2 cups of the whipping cream in a small bowl and beat until stiff. Refrigerate until needed.

In the top of a double boiler, heat the remaining 1/2 cup whipping cream with the white chocolate over moderate heat, stirring frequently, just until the chocolate has melted. Remove from the heat and transfer to a large bowl. Add the marshmallow cream, crème de cacao, vanilla extract, and black pepper. Beat until thoroughly combined and very smooth. Fold in the reserved whipped cream and mix gently just until combined.

Spoon the mixture into individual 1-cup molds or into one large mold or shallow bowl. Cover surface with parchment or waxed paper, then with foil, and place in freezer until set, about 6 hours. Remove from molds by running hot water around the outside of the container. Flip over onto plates and garnish with fresh mint sprigs. Serve immediately.

strawberry-blackberry sorbet with pink and black peppercorns

1/4 cup fresh lemon juice

2 tablespoons blackberry (or other berry-flavored) liqueur

1 envelope unflavored gelatin

1/2 cup water

1 pint strawberries, stemmed and coarsely chopped

1 pint blackberries

3/4 to 1 cup sugar (depending on the sweetness of the berries)

1 tablespoon pink peppercorns, slightly crushed

1/2 teaspoon finely ground black peppercorns

Fresh mint sprigs, for garnish

➤ Ruby red and saturated with the flavor essence of berries, this peppercorn-flecked iced confection will thrill the taste buds and delight the eye. Serve as a palate refresher between courses, or with thin butter cookies for a summertime dessert.

HOT 3

makes 4 to 6 servings

Place the lemon juice and blackberry liqueur in a large bowl and mix well. Sprinkle the gelatin over the lemon juice mixture. Heat the water in a small saucepan until hot but not boiling. Add the water to the lemon juice–gelatin mixture, and mix well until gelatin is thoroughly dissolved.

To the gelatin mixture add the berries, sugar, and peppercorns; mix well. Using a blender, purée in batches until smooth. Strain through a fine wire mesh or sieve two times, or until no seeds remain. Transfer to a plastic container with a tight-fitting lid and place in the freezer for at least 6 hours. If you prefer an ultra-smooth texture, stir the mixture approximately once an hour during the first three hours of freezing.

To serve, remove from the freezer about 5 minutes before serving. When softened slightly, scoop into small balls using a melon baller or into larger balls using a small ice-cream scoop. Garnish with fresh mint sprigs and serve immediately.

horseradish

◆　◆　◆　◆　◆　**HORSERADISH**

Horseradish is a cherished condiment in many parts of the world; some cuisines greatly depend upon the pungent root to add a distinguishing note and character to their foods. Until recently, however, Americans associated the sinus-clearing root with but two dishes: prime rib and baked potatoes. The rage for hot, spicy foods has changed that, bringing both fresh and prepared horseradish new popularity.

A member of the *Cruciferae* family, horseradish is a perennial plant native to eastern Europe and western Asia. It now grows in Britain, Russia, northern Europe, and the United States. The plant has long, dark green leaves that can be used in salads and other savory dishes, but it is the root that appears most frequently in prepared foods and condiments.

Approximately the size of a half-dollar in circumference, the ten- to twelve-inch-long root is rough and knobby, with pale yellow to light brown skin tone and ivory-colored, slightly fibrous flesh. Fresh roots must be carefully scrubbed under running warm water with a vegetable brush to remove caked-on dirt. Once cleaned, use a sharp paring knife to remove the thin outer skin. At this point you may either grate, finely mince, dice, julienne, or coarsely chop the root.

When buying fresh horseradish, look for hard, relatively unblemished roots that do not yield to bending motions (rubbery roots are past their prime and short on flavor). To store fresh horseradish, loosely wrap in paper towels, place inside a plastic bag, and store in the refrigerator for up to one-and-a-half months. Some people prefer storing the root inside a paper bag, but I feel the additional plastic wrapping provides better protection. Once opened, jars of prepared horseradish begin to lose their potency. Store the condiment in the refrigerator for up to five months.

To finely mince horseradish, as called for in the recipes, slice the peeled root into very thin rounds. Spread the slices on a cutting board and, using a sharp chef's knife or a cleaver, chop into tiny pieces no larger than $\frac{1}{16}$ inch. Remember, when preparing fresh horseradish, open the window closest to your work area to allow the pungent fumes to escape.

Fresh horseradish root imparts the greatest essence when grated. It lends a generous amount of flavor when finely minced, and a moderate quantity when diced or coarsely chopped. Like many fresh ingredients, horseradish is most potent in its raw form. Retaining a moderate amount of flavor when heated, fresh horseradish root, prepared horseradish, and wasabi lose most of their intensity when cooked for extended periods of time. For this reason, add the ingredient toward the end of cooking for a pronounced flavor, or after a dish has completely cooled for the most dramatic effect.

Dishes from this chapter use both fresh horseradish and bottled "regular" and "cream-style" horse-radish. I think you'll find using the fresh root exhilarating, but if you can't readily find it in your local produce shop or grocery store, feel free to use the bottled variety instead. Refer to the grated measures on the chart at right when substituting bottled for the fresh.

This chapter contains a recipe that uses wasabi, the pungent green paste referred to as "Japanese horseradish." Like European horseradish, wasabi can deliver a devastating blow to the sinuses. As a matter of fact, American hotheads often show off their heat tolerance by the high ratio of wasabi to soy sauce they mix for their sushi and sashimi.

A type of aquatic plant indigenous to Japan, wasabi comes from an edible root with pale green flesh. Like horseradish, the root must first be peeled before the flesh is grated, minced, or chopped and used for eating or cooking. Although wasabi is rarely available fresh in this country, it is sold in small tins in powdered form or as a paste in tubes. The powder must be mixed with cold water to form a paste or thin sauce before it is used; to allow the flavor to develop, let it stand at room temperature for about 10 minutes before serving or using in a recipe. The paste can be used directly from the tube.

The recipes in this chapter range from super-mild dishes, such as *Fried Egg and Potato Hash with Horseradish,* to the raging-hot *Horseradish Cream Cheese–Stuffed Cucumbers.* The *Iced Cucumber-Horseradish Soup* is both incendiary and frigid—a startling sensation for the palate, indeed.

Although many of the dishes are naturally low in fat, *Poached Tofu and Green Beans with Wasabi Glaze* and *Tomato and Cucumber Aspic with Horseradish* are particularly so. Don't save the *Rye Bread Stuffing with Toasted Almonds and Horseradish* only for holiday cooking—its irresistible bold flavor and win-ning texture are pleasing year-round. Although there is a tempting variety of dishes, there are no desserts in this chapter; I like to stretch, not break, gustatory boundaries!

These recipes call for the fresh root in inch lengths, but since roots vary slightly in size, it is impossible to obtain exact measurements for recipes. As with ginger root, precision is not critical. Although I have suggested quantities, adjust the amounts of horseradish called for in recipes to suit your personal taste.

1- to 2-inch piece fresh horseradish root = about 1/4 cup grated, 1/2 cup minced

2- to 3-inch piece fresh horseradish root = about 1/2 cup grated, 3/4 cup minced

5- to 6-inch piece fresh horseradish root = about 1 cup grated, 1 1/4 cups minced

iced cucumber-horseradish soup

3 large cucumbers, peeled
and coarsely chopped

1 small bunch scallions,
trimmed and coarsely
chopped

4-inch piece fresh
horseradish root, peeled
and finely chopped

4 cups plain low-fat yogurt

Salt and pepper, to taste

¹/₄ cup minced fresh chives
and/or finely chopped mint,
for garnish

Cracked ice, optional

➤ At once frigid and
fiery, this soup is for hard-core
horseradish fiends—and
only those who enjoy large
intercranial explosions!

HOTTEST 10

makes about 6 servings

In a large bowl, combine the cucumber, scallions, horseradish, and yogurt; mix well. Using a blender, purée in batches until very smooth. Season with salt and pepper. Transfer to a nonreactive container, cover tightly, and refrigerate for at least 6 hours or up to 24 hours.

To serve, ladle into chilled cups or shallow bowls and garnish with chives and/or fresh mint. You may add a couple of tablespoons of finely cracked ice to each bowl to add to the visual effect and to further reduce the temperature of the soup.

tomato and cucumber aspic with horseradish

Place the water in a large bowl. Sprinkle the gelatin over the surface and let stand, undisturbed, 5 to 7 minutes at room temperature.

In a medium saucepan, heat the tomato juice, shallots, and honey over moderate heat until the mixture just begins to boil. Add 1 cup of the tomato juice to the gelatin mixture, stirring constantly to dissolve the gelatin. Slowly add the remaining tomato juice, stirring constantly. Cool to room temperature. When cool, add the horseradish and bell pepper; mix well. Season with salt and pepper. Pour into mold(s) and refrigerate 4 to 6 hours, or until completely set.

To unmold: Set the gelatin molds in a pan filled with hot water for 30 seconds, or until the sides just begin to soften. Remove the pan from the water. Place a flat plate or platter firmly over the surface of the molds and, using one swift movement, flip the two over together, so the aspic is transferred onto the plate. Serve immediately.

➤ Serve this powerful jelled "Bloody Mary" for brunch or lunch with a tossed green salad or German-style potato salad.

Make the aspic in attractive, individual gelatin molds or in one four-cup mold, or double the recipe and use a large eight-cup mold. Individual one-cup capacity angel food cake pans make a particularly handsome presentation—even more dramatic when the center contains a shot of iced vodka!

HOTTEST 7

makes 4 servings

¹/₃ cup cold water

2 envelopes unflavored gelatin

2¹/₂ cups tomato juice

2 shallots, trimmed and thinly sliced

1¹/₂ tablespoons honey

¹/₃ cup prepared horseradish

1 medium green bell pepper, cut into small triangles

Salt and pepper, to taste

horseradish-sesame rice balls with cucumber

3 cups homemade vegetable stock (page 13) or canned vegetable broth (preferably low-sodium)

1 1/2 tablespoons unsalted butter

1 cup medium-grain pearl rice

1/3 cup teriyaki sauce

1 1/2 tablespoons prepared cream-style horseradish

Salt and pepper, to taste

1 small cucumber, peeled, halved, seeded, and cut into 1/2-inch dice

1 to 1 1/2 cups sesame seeds, for coating balls

➤ Garnished with bell peppers cut into fanciful shapes, these feisty cucumber-filled rice balls make a terrific hors d'oeuvre for a formal cocktail party. Drizzled with sour cream or served on a bed of lightly dressed Asian greens, they make an outstanding first course.

If you'd like to double-up on the horseradish for additional firepower, substitute a diced chunk of fresh horseradish root for the cucumber, or use both, cutting each of them smaller to accommodate the size of the rice ball.

HOTTEST 7

makes 12 balls; 4 to 6 servings

In a medium saucepan, bring the vegetable stock and butter to boil over high heat. Add the rice and return to the boil, stirring frequently. Reduce the heat to moderately low, cover, and cook 15 minutes. Remove cover and cook an additional 7 or 8 minutes, or until all the liquid has been absorbed and the rice is very tender. Cool to room temperature.

To the rice add the teriyaki sauce and horseradish. Season with salt and pepper and mix well.

Form the mixture into a 15-inch-long cylinder. Cut into twelve equal pieces and form each into a ball. Use your finger to press a cucumber dice into the center of each ball; close over the hole with the rice, forming a smooth ball. Roll each ball in the sesame seeds, taking care to evenly coat all sides. Cover tightly and refrigerate for at least 1 hour and up to 3 hours. Serve slightly chilled.

poached tofu and green beans with wasabi glaze

To make the wasabi glaze, in a small bowl, combine the wasabi powder and vinegar; mix well to form a smooth paste. Add the peanut oil, teriyaki sauce, and sesame oil; mix well and set aside.

Place the block of tofu on a flat surface. Cut in half lengthwise. Cut each half into 4 equal sections. Using 3 green beans per tofu square, carefully insert the beans through the center and out the other side of each square, so that the tips are exposed on either side.

In a large skillet, bring the vegetable stock to boil over moderate heat. Add the tofu squares, cover, and cook 2 to 3 minutes per side, or until the tofu is slightly tender to the touch. Remove with a slotted spatula and drain on paper towels. The tofu either can be served immediately or covered and refrigerated until chilled, up to 3 hours. Drizzle with the glaze and garnish with the sesame seeds before serving.

➤ Firm tofu and green beans form a striking visual presentation in this low-fat, Japanese-inspired dish. It makes a stunning first course or, paired with ginger-accented buckwheat noodles or miso-laced rice, a healthful and elegant main course.

HOT 2

makes about 4 servings

WASABI GLAZE:

¹/₄ cup wasabi powder

2 tablespoons seasoned rice wine vinegar

2 tablespoons peanut oil

1 tablespoon teriyaki sauce

¹/₂ teaspoon Asian sesame oil

14 ounces firm tofu (1 block)

24 small thin green beans (about ¹/₂ pound), blanched

2 cups homemade vegetable stock (page 13) or canned vegetable broth (preferably low-sodium)

Black sesame seeds, for garnish

horseradish cream cheese–stuffed cucumbers

2 large cucumbers, peeled

8 ounces natural cream cheese, softened to room temperature

4-inch piece fresh horserad-ish root, peeled and minced

Salt and pepper, to taste

1 bunch fresh chives, halved, for garnish

➤ Present this festive low-calorie dish with toasted pita bread for a hot-weather appetizer or first course.

HOTTER 6

makes about 5 servings

Place the cucumber on a cutting board. Position the knife on one tip of the cucumber at a 45-degree angle and cut through. Move the knife about 1½ inches down and make a cut straight across the cucumber, so that you have a 1½-inch-long section of cucumber with one straight end and one angled end. Continue cutting both cucumbers in this fashion, alternating the 45-degree angle cut and the straight-across cut. You should have approximately ten sections from the two cucumbers.

Using a small spoon, starting from the angled end remove the seeds and pulp from the center of each section, leaving a thin layer of flesh on the bottom of the straight end to prevent the fill-ing from falling out the bottom. Gently dry the insides of each piece with a paper towel.

In a small bowl using an electric mixer, beat the cream cheese and horseradish until thoroughly combined, soft, and fluffy. Season with salt and pepper.

Fill each cucumber section with the cream cheese–horseradish mixture, dividing equally. Make small bundles using three or four chives per cucumber section, and anchor the cut ends of the bundle straight up into the cream cheese in each. Serve immediately.

potato-horseradish croquettes

Preheat oven to 400° F.

Bake the potatoes in the center of the oven 50 to 55 minutes, or until very tender when pierced with a fork. Remove from the oven and cool to room temperature. Halve potatoes lengthwise and, using a fork, gently scrape pulp into a large bowl. Add the scallions, horseradish, and whole egg and stir well with a fork (to prevent the mixture from becoming gummy). Season well with salt and pepper. Cover and refrigerate for at least 2 hours or up to 8 hours.

To shape the croquettes, using about 2 rounded tablespoons per croquette, form the chilled potato mixture into small balls. Place the beaten eggs in a shallow bowl, and the bread crumbs in a pie plate or shallow baking dish. Dip each croquette into the beaten eggs, taking care to completely cover. Gently roll in the bread crumbs, again taking care to completely cover each croquette. Set aside on a pan lightly dusted with bread crumbs. (Although the croquettes are best cooked right away, if you are pressed for time, you may cover them loosely and refrigerate for up to 3 hours before cooking.)

In a large, shallow-sided pot, heat 2 cups of the oil over moderately high heat until very hot, but not smoking. Add the croquettes in batches (do not crowd or they will not cook properly), and fry, turning as they brown, until toasty brown on all sides. Remove with a slotted spoon and drain on paper towels. Cook the remaining croquettes in this fashion, adding more oil to the pot as needed, and letting it heat to the correct temperature before adding more croquettes. After draining on paper towels, the cooked croquettes may be kept warm on a baking sheet in a 250° F. oven for 7 or 8 minutes before serving. Serve warm, garnished with sprigs of chives or fresh herbs.

➤ These little savory nuggets are irresistible, especially when served with ice-cold ale. Accompany the croquettes with sautéed mixed vegetables or a cold vegetable platter for a full meal.

HOT 3

makes 22 croquettes; 6 to 8 servings

2 large baking potatoes (about 1³/₄ pounds)

4 scallions, trimmed and finely chopped

5-inch piece fresh horseradish, peeled and minced

1 whole egg, plus 2 eggs, lightly beaten

Salt and pepper, to taste

1¹/₂ cups finely ground dried bread crumbs

2¹/₂ to 3 cups vegetable oil, for frying

Fresh chives or herb sprigs, for garnish

grilled smoked cheddar cheese sandwiches with horseradish and tomato

2 to 3 tablespoons prepared cream-style horseradish

2 large slices good-quality, firm whole-wheat or rye bread

¼ pound smoked Cheddar cheese, thinly sliced

3 thin slices tomato

1 tablespoon peanut or vegetable oil (approximately), for cooking

➤ This recipe gives directions for making one large sandwich. It easily can be increased in quantity to fit your needs, which may be greater than initially planned once you taste this flavor-packed lunch treat.

HOTTER 4

makes 1 sandwich; 1 serving

Spread the horseradish on one side of each bread slice. Cover the horseradish on one slice with half of the cheese. Top with the tomatoes and cover with the remaining cheese. Cover with the second slice of bread, horseradish-side down. Press gently to secure the sandwich.

In a small sauté pan, heat half of the oil over moderately low heat until warm. Add the sandwich, cover, and cook on one side until the bread is toasty brown and the cheese begins to melt, 4 or 5 minutes. Using a spatula, carefully flip the sandwich over; add the remaining ½ tablespoon oil (you may need to add more oil if the pan is very dry, and the bread is absorbing a lot of oil). Cook second side 4 or 5 minutes, or until all the cheese has melted and the bread is toasty brown. Remove and drain on paper towels, if necessary. Serve immediately.

fried egg and potato hash with horseradish

4 medium red or white
potatoes (about 2 pounds),
cut into 1/2-inch dice

3 tablespoons peanut or
vegetable oil

4-inch piece fresh
horseradish, peeled and
finely chopped

1 green bell pepper, cut
into small dice

3 tablespoons prepared
cream-style horseradish

8 eggs

➤ This palate-stimulating
breakfast or brunch dish will
send a wake-up call to even the
most tired taste buds. To complete the meal, serve with
buttered rye toast and glasses
of tomato juice.

HOT 3

makes 4 servings

In a very large, nonstick sauté pan, cook the potatoes in 2 tablespoons of the oil over moderately high heat 10 to 12 minutes until golden brown, stirring frequently. Add the fresh horseradish and bell pepper and cook 2 minutes, stirring constantly. Add the prepared horseradish and mix well. Transfer to an ovenproof dish and keep warm in a 250° F. oven.

Taking care to leave the yolks intact, crack the eggs into a large bowl. Heat the remaining tablespoon of oil in the sauté pan over moderate heat. When the oil is hot but not smoking, pour in all of the eggs, again taking care to keep yolks intact as you add them to the pan. Cook the eggs until set on underside, then gently flip to cook second side (it's okay if a few yolks break). Alternatively, you may cover the eggs and cook without flipping over moderately low heat until set. (Using this method they won't have as much "fried egg" taste, texture, or appearance; it's a matter of your preference.)

Add the eggs to the potato-horseradish mixture and mix gently (the yolks will break and create a delicious golden "sauce"). Serve immediately.

rye bread stuffing with toasted almonds and horseradish

In a very large sauté pan, cook the onion and spices in the butter and olive oil over moderate heat 10 minutes, stirring frequently. Add the fresh horseradish and cook 5 minutes, stirring occasionally. Add the bread and increase heat to high. Cook, stirring constantly, 2 to 3 minutes or until bread begins to brown. Add the vegetable stock and cook 3 to 5 minutes, stirring occasionally, until about 2 tablespoons of liquid remain.

Remove from the heat, stir in the prepared horseradish and the almonds, and season with salt and pepper.

May be served immediately or, if you prefer the top browned, transfer to an ovenproof dish, dot with butter, and bake on the upper shelf of a 400° F. oven until golden brown, about 12 minutes.

➤ I relish the combined flavors and textures of horseradish, toasted almonds, and caraway seeds in this classic stuffing-with-a-twist.

Use as a filling for winter squash, zucchini, and eggplant, or serve as is with a drizzle of tomato sauce or a dollop of sour cream.

HOT 2

makes 4 to 6 servings

1 large onion, cut into medium dice

2 teaspoons *each* ground fenugreek and fennel seeds

3 tablespoons unsalted butter

1 1/2 tablespoons olive oil

5-inch piece fresh horseradish root, peeled and minced

10 slices stale rye bread (preferably sourdough), cut into 1/2-inch cubes

2 cups homemade vegetable stock (page 13) or canned vegetable broth (preferably low-sodium)

2 tablespoons prepared cream-style horseradish

1 cup toasted almonds, coarsely chopped

Salt and pepper, to taste

chilies

Chili peppers are by far the most familiar source of culinary heat. They are also the most adored. The fact that fresh and dried chilies range from mild to scorching hot is a mixed blessing. I'm sure hotheads would prefer each and every chili pepper to be blazing hot, but food lovers with tamer tastes enjoy and exploit the variations among them.

To further complicate matters for the cook, however, heat levels also fluctuate among peppers of the same type. For example: you buy six poblano chilies to roast and stuff—four are moderately hot; two are nearly impossible to eat. Depending on their palates, some of your dining guests will be exceedingly happy, others may plead for mercy.

The recipes in this chapter also vary in intensity. Not all are blistering hot—some are rather benign. These dishes can be made hotter simply by using more chilies, but you run the risk of obliterating all the other flavors. Fire and drama are good, and certain foods automatically call out for extremes of this type, but other dishes crave a more gentle approach. *Roasted Chili Pepper Nuts* and *Potato-Cheese Tacos with Three Chilies* are relatively temperate rather than extreme. Also moderate in terms of heat, but loaded with flavor, are the *Spring Vegetable Stir-Fry with Mild and Hot Chilies; Baked Polenta with Chili Peppers and Smoked Cheese;* and *Golden Masa Cakes with Fresh and Dried Chili Peppers.*

The *Five-Alarm Gazpacho* easily can be reduced to a two-alarm fire or expanded to a ten-alarm blaze. If you haven't yet sampled the hottest chili pepper of all—the habanero—and you like Mexican-style salsa, try the *Flaming-Hot Habanero Chili Pepper Sauce.* Mind you, it isn't the kind of salsa you slather on quesadillas, tacos, or enchiladas but rather the sort you prudently drizzle onto your food for a dazzling spark of flavor.

The hottest thing I've ever put in my mouth is the white bean dish included here called *Angelic Beans with Sauce of the Devil.* It not only features the torrid habanero, it calls for sixteen of them! You don't have to use the full amount, but if you enjoy explosive sensations, follow the recipe quantities.

Chilies also are unexpectedly delicious in desserts. If you've never experienced the marriage of bittersweet chocolate and fresh or dried chili peppers, you're in for a treat. I'm especially fond of dried ancho or pasilla chilies in combination with bittersweet, semisweet, or milk chocolate. There is something about the dark, dusky, mellow flavor of dried chilies blended with chocolate that makes them a match made in heaven—at least to my palate. The *Frozen Chocolate Silk with Ancho Chilies* demonstrates this affinity; voluptuous and creamy, it still packs a punch.

Historical evidence suggests that chili peppers were a common cooking ingredient as early as 4000 B.C. Aztecs and Mayans in Central and South America and Indians in the West Indies had used fresh chilies for centuries, but it wasn't until Columbus's second journey in 1495 that chili peppers were introduced to the Old World. Spanish explorers returned home with the plant, where it thrived in the hot, sunny climate of the Mediterranean. Portuguese and Spanish traders spread the chili pepper on their travels to Africa, India, and the Far East, where it was quickly assimilated into the native cuisines. By the 1600s chili peppers had been introduced to virtually every region of the world.

Native to South America, chili peppers are now cultivated in India, Mexico, China, Indonesia, Thailand, and the United States, where New Mexico, Texas, California, Arizona, and Louisiana are the leading growers. Typically, chilies grow best in hot, humid climates with long growing seasons, but many varieties also do well in mild, temperate zones.

It is difficult to differentiate and classify the hundreds of varieties of chili peppers. Deviations within individual classes make it even harder to predict the level of heat contained within a given chili pepper. Since the capsicum, contained primarily in the veins and seeds, dictates overall heat level, one way to determine the fire potential of a chili is by counting its veins and examining the quantity of seeds. Generally speaking, fruits with a higher ratio of veins and seeds to flesh are hotter than those with proportionately fewer veins and seeds. Additionally, those grown in hotter climates tend to be a bit more fiery.

In 1902, pharmacologist Wilber Scoville developed a method for measuring the amount, or power, of capsicum in a given pepper. Originally, Scoville presented tasters with a mixture of ground chilies, sugar, alcohol, and water. Values were given according to the amount of diluting ingredients (sugar, alcohol, and water) necessary to make the mixture devoid of heat. Today computers perform this challenging task, rating peppers by Scoville Units, which indicate parts per million of capsicum.

The Scoville scale begins at zero with mild bell peppers and moves into the lower mid-range, with the cascabel rating four (out of ten) and a unit measurement of 1,500 to 2,500. The common and relatively benign jalapeño ranks dead center with a unit rating of 2,500 to 5,000. Cayenne, tabasco, aji, and piquin peppers, packed with approximately 30,000 to 50,000 Scoville Units, rank number eight out of ten. The scale tops off with the wicked and much-prized habanero and Bahamian chilies, which contain between 100,000 and 300,000 Scoville Units.

With over four hundred varieties being grown today, the availability and assortment of fresh and dried chili peppers are staggering. Some of the more commonly available fresh chilies include jalapeño, serrano, poblano, and yellow wax, but bird's eye (or Thai), habanero, cherry, and cayenne chili peppers are now stocked by many grocery stores and produce markets as well. Dried chili peppers are also becoming more widely available in full-service grocery stores—especially those with Latin or ethnic food sections. Most every dried chili pepper called for in this book can be found in Latin American grocery stores or produce markets. Many of the fresh varieties also are sold in stores featuring foods of Latin America, the Caribbean, and Africa. Asian markets also carry a wide range of fresh chili peppers, and usually one or two dried types. If you cannot find the exact type of pepper called for in the following recipes, substitute one of similar size, color, and approximate heat intensity.

When purchasing fresh chili peppers, look for fruit that is firm, smooth, free of blemishes, and even colored. Store fresh chilies in a plastic bag in the refrigerator for up to two weeks. If your purchases begin to show signs of age and you have no immediate use for them, roast, peel, seed, and stem the chilies and either store in the freezer in a tightly sealed container for up to ten months, or cover with peanut or olive oil and store in a tightly sealed container in the refrigerator for up to two months. Alternatively, you can "pickle" the roasted peppers by covering them with a mild vinegar, or marinate them with a mixture of oil and vinegar and even some garlic and herbs.

Dried peppers should be glossy and free of holes, tears, and insects (some prepackaged dried chili peppers imported from Mexico come with unexpected extras: tiny flying insects). Store dried chili peppers in tightly sealed plastic or paper bags in a cool, dark place for up to one year; six months is optimal. To rehydrate, place the chilies in a bowl and cover with hot or warm water (top with a smaller bowl filled with water to keep them submerged). Soak at room temperature until soft and pliable. Depending on the type of chili, this could take as little as fifteen minutes or as long as three hours.

To avoid contact with the volatile oils in fresh and dried chili peppers, please wear gloves when preparing them for cooking. If you must handle the chilies with your bare hands, I strongly urge you to refrain from touching *any* mucus membranes until you're certain your hands are free from the natural oils. Unfortunately, repeated hand washing with hot water and soap will not fully remove the capsicum-containing oils.

If a chili pepper launches an attack on your palate beyond what is comfortably painful, try a big slurp of milk or a spoonful of yogurt or even sour cream. Plain rice, bread, and tortillas—*not water*—also will come to the rescue.

roasted chili pepper nuts

10 ounces macadamia nuts

8 ounces pistachio nuts

8 ounces almonds

8 ounces pumpkin seeds

4 ancho chili peppers

4 dried cayenne or chiltepe chili peppers

3 dried cascabel chili peppers

2 dried guajillo or New Mexico chili peppers

1 chipotle chili pepper

1 1/2 tablespoons Hungarian paprika

2 tablespoons kosher salt, or to taste

1 1/2 tablespoons ground cumin

3 tablespoons olive oil

2 tablespoons unsalted butter, melted

➤ Serve these spiced nuts as hors d'oeuvres or snacks with cocktails, beer, or soft drinks. Finely chopped, they make a great topping for casserole dishes, sautéed mixed vegetables, or tossed green salads.

This particular combination of nuts forms a balanced, well-rounded blend of flavors, but feel free to substitute your favorite nuts for one or two of the types specified in the recipe.

HOTTER 5

makes about 3 1/2 cups

Preheat oven to 325° F. Place nuts and pumpkin seeds in a large mixing bowl. Set aside.

Arrange the ancho, cayenne, cascabel, guajillo, and chipotle chili peppers on a baking sheet. Roast 3 to 5 minutes or until aromatic, puffy, and a shade darker. Remove from the oven and cool to room temperature. Remove stems and seeds and discard. Using an electric spice grinder, pulverize the chilies in batches to a fine powder. Add to the nuts along with the paprika, salt, and cumin; mix well. Drizzle the oil and butter over the nuts and mix well.

Divide the nuts between two baking sheets, making a single layer on each. Bake in the oven 25 to 27 minutes, rotating pans between shelves and stirring the nuts from time to time. Remove from the oven and cool to room temperature. Serve immediately or store in tightly sealed plastic bags in the refrigerator for up to 3 weeks. Bring to room temperature before serving.

flaming-hot habanero chili pepper sauce

In a large, nonstick sauté pan, cook the onion and garlic over high heat 5 minutes, stirring frequently. Add the chili peppers and cook 5 to 7 minutes, stirring frequently, until the onions are blackened around the edges and the chilies are limp. Add the water and vinegar, reduce heat to moderately high, and cook 5 minutes. Remove from heat and cool slightly.

Transfer to a food processor and process, pulsing on and off, until uniformly minced. Season with salt and pepper and add cilantro, if desired. Store in a tightly sealed nonreactive container in the refrigerator up to 1 month.

➤ Although this is one of the most fierce chili pepper sauces I have sampled, it also has a tremendous amount of flavor and depth. Remember: *a little bit goes a long way!* Spoon a little on fried or scrambled eggs, or use it to add pizzazz to rice, pasta, or grain dishes.

HOTTEST 10+

makes about 1 ½ cups

1 large onion, halved and thinly sliced

5 cloves garlic

12 habanero chili peppers, stemmed

4 thick cayenne or hot goat horn chili peppers, stemmed and coarsely chopped

2 pimento or apple chili peppers, stemmed and coarsely chopped

1 cup water

1/4 cup white wine vinegar or apple cider vinegar

Salt and pepper, to taste

1/3 cup minced fresh cilantro, optional

corn pudding with sweet and hot chilies

3 large ears corn, kernels shaved (about 2 1/2 cups corn kernels)

3 hot cherry chili peppers, stemmed, seeded, and coarsely chopped

2 Hungarian sweet chili peppers, stemmed and coarsely chopped

2 bird's eye (Thai) chili peppers, stemmed and finely chopped

3 tablespoons unsalted butter

2 teaspoons dried chili powder

1 teaspoon minced chipotle chili pepper

1 1/4 cups heavy whipping cream

3 eggs, separated

2 teaspoons kosher or sea salt

1 teaspoon black pepper

➤ How can you go wrong with a dish that contains mild and hot chili peppers, fresh sweet corn, and cream? If you're like me, you may find it difficult to keep yourself from eating the entire dish. Serve with sliced tomatoes garnished with fresh basil or a summer vegetable salad of steamed sugar snap peas, English green peas, and asparagus.

HOTTER 6

makes 4 to 6 servings

Preheat oven to 350° F. Generously grease a 2-quart ovenproof baking dish.

Place the corn in a large bowl. In a large sauté pan, heat the hot cherry, Hungarian, and bird's eye chili peppers over high heat 1½ to 2 minutes, until any liquid has evaporated and they are slightly limp. Add the butter and stir until melted. Remove from the heat and add to the corn, along with the chili powder, chipotle, whipping cream, egg yolks, salt, and pepper; mix well.

Using an electric mixer, beat the egg whites in a medium bowl until stiff but not dry. Gently fold into the corn mixture just until blended. Do not overmix. Turn mixture into prepared dish.

Set the baking dish in a large, ovenproof pan. Add hot water until it reaches halfway up the side of the pan. Place in the center of the oven and bake 45 to 50 minutes, or until a knife inserted into the center comes out clean. Remove from the oven and let stand at room temperature 5 to 7 minutes before serving.

five-alarm gazpacho

rrange a single layer of the tomatoes, cut sides down, in a large, nonstick sauté pan. Add half of the onion and sprinkle with 1 teaspoon of the salt. Cook over high heat until cut sides of tomatoes are slightly charred, 4 to 6 minutes. Remove the mixture from the pan and place in a large bowl. Repeat with the remaining tomatoes, red onion, and salt and add to the bowl.

Add the cucumber, red bell pepper, chili peppers, garlic, vinegars, and olive oil to the bowl and mix well. Let stand at room temperature for 30 minutes to 1 hour. Stir in the water.

Using a blender, purée half the mixture and strain through a fine wire mesh or sieve. Transfer to a storage container large enough to accommodate the entire batch of soup. Purée the remaining mixture with the croutons and add to the strained mixture. Mix well and season with additional salt (if necessary) and pepper. If serving immediately, add 1 cup crushed ice and mix until thoroughly melted. Alternatively, refrigerate until well chilled. Garnish with green bell pepper or chives before serving.

➤ This recipe produces a slightly thick, semichunky gazpacho. If you prefer a completely smooth version, strain both batches of soup after puréeing in the blender and omit the croutons. Conversely, if you prefer a soup with lots of body, purée the mixture along with the croutons, but omit straining it altogether.

HOTTEST 8

makes 6 to 8 servings

1 1/2 pounds ripe Roma tomatoes, halved lengthwise

1 medium red onion, thinly sliced

2 teaspoons kosher salt

1 large cucumber, peeled, seeded, and coarsely chopped

1 red bell pepper, coarsely chopped

3 bird's eye (Thai) chili peppers, stemmed and coarsely chopped

2 jalapeño chili peppers, stemmed and coarsely chopped

2 cloves garlic, coarsely chopped

3 tablespoons red wine vinegar

2 tablespoons sherry vinegar

1/4 cup extra-virgin olive oil

1 cup ice water

1 cup croutons or prepared unseasoned stuffing mix

Black pepper, to taste

1 green bell pepper, cut into tiny dice, or 1/2 cup minced chives, for garnish

spring vegetable stir-fry with mild and hot chilies

Bring a small pot of salted water to boil over high heat. Remove the fava beans from the shell (you should have about 1 cup). Add the beans to the water and cook 2 minutes. Drain in a colander and cool to room temperature. Using your fingers, gently snip the outer skin on the tip of each fava bean; gently squeeze the bean from the outer skin. Discard skins and set fava beans aside.

In a very large sauté pan, cook the asparagus and sugar peas in the olive oil over moderate heat for 3 minutes, stirring occasionally. Add the chili peppers, fava beans, and sherry and cook over high heat 2 to 3 minutes, or until all the vegetables are tender. Add the garlic chives and vinegar and cook 15 to 20 seconds, stirring constantly. Season with salt and pepper and serve immediately.

➤ This is a lovely dish to serve on a warm spring or summer evening. Accompany with warm rolls and butter and an oaky chardonnay or chilled sherry.

HOT 1

makes 4 to 6 servings

1¹/₂ pounds fresh fava beans in the shell

1 pound asparagus, bottoms trimmed, sliced on the diagonal into 1-inch-long pieces

³/₄ pound sugar snap peas, ends trimmed and stringed

1¹/₂ tablespoons olive oil

3 apple or small pimento chili peppers, stemmed, seeded, and quartered

2 red jalapeño or hot cherry chili peppers, stemmed, seeded, and thinly sliced

3 tablespoons dry sherry

1 bunch garlic chives or scallions, finely chopped

Splash sherry vinegar or champagne vinegar

Salt and pepper, to taste

chili pepper–stuffed mushroom caps

21 large, very fresh
mushrooms

2 tablespoons olive oil

2 tablespoons unsalted butter

2 cloves garlic, minced

2 bird's eye (Thai) chili
peppers, stemmed and finely
chopped

2 apple or small pimento
chili peppers, stemmed,
seeded, and finely chopped

2 hot goat horn or New
Mexico chili peppers,
stemmed, seeded, and finely
chopped

1 Hungarian sweet chili
pepper, stemmed, seeded,
and finely chopped

1 1/2 teaspoons *each* dried
thyme and sage

1/3 cup dry vermouth

1 1/3 cups finely ground dried
bread crumbs

1 1/2 tablespoons sherry
vinegar

Salt and pepper, to taste

➤ Hotheads and mushroom-lovers alike will enjoy this chili pepper–enhanced classic hors d'oeuvre.

Although they already pack a punch, for even more heat, use only bird's eye (Thai) chili peppers instead of the mixture suggested.

HOTTER 6

makes 18 mushrooms; 4 to 6 servings

Preheat oven to 400° F. Lightly grease a very shallow baking pan (a jelly roll pan is ideal).

Remove stems from 18 of the mushrooms and reserve caps. Finely chop the stems along with the 3 remaining mushrooms and set aside.

In a large sauté pan, heat the olive oil and butter over moderately high heat. Add the chopped mushrooms, garlic, chili peppers, and herbs. Increase the heat to high and cook 10 minutes, stirring frequently, until very soft and all the liquid has evaporated. Add the vermouth and cook 1 to 2 minutes, or until the liquid has almost evaporated. Add the bread crumbs and cook 3 minutes, stirring constantly, until lightly browned. Add the vinegar, salt, and pepper and mix well. Remove from the heat and cool to room temperature. (If the mixture seems too dry at this point you may add a little melted butter or olive oil.)

Tightly pack the cavity of each mushroom cap with the bread crumb mixture, rounding it into a dome shape. Place the mushrooms on the prepared pan, stuffed sides up, leaving approximately 3/4 inch between each one. Bake in the center of the oven 8 to 10 minutes, or until the mushrooms are tender and the filling is hot. Remove from the oven and serve immediately.

golden masa cakes with fresh and dried chili peppers

Soak the ancho and chipotle chilies in warm water to cover 1 to 1½ hours, or until soft and pliable. Finely chop and set aside.

In a large bowl, combine the *masa harina*, chili powder, salt, and baking powder. Add the water, cayenne chilies, and reserved chopped chilies. Mix well with a large fork until a dough forms. Add the cheese and mix with your hands to thoroughly combine ingredients and form a smooth, pliable dough. Shape the dough into a long cylinder, approximately 1 inch in diameter. Wrap tightly in plastic wrap and refrigerate for at least 2 hours, or up to 8 hours.

Thirty minutes prior to cooking, remove dough from refrigerator and slice into 20 equal pieces. When pliable, use your hands to pat each piece into a small cake.

In a large, nonstick sauté pan, heat about ½ inch of oil over moderate heat until hot but not smoking. Arrange a single layer of masa cakes in the oil, leaving approximately ¾ inch of space between each one. Cook until golden brown on bottoms, 3 or 4 minutes. Gently flip cakes using a spatula, and cook second sides until golden brown. Remove with slotted spatula and drain on paper towels. Cook remaining cakes in this fashion, adding more oil as needed. Serve immediately, garnished with sprigs of cilantro.

➤ For lunch or a light supper, pair these tasty little cakes with a salad of finely shredded cabbage, carrots, and red onions spiked with vinegar and dried oregano. For an hors d'oeuvre, serve with a platter of assorted Mexican cheeses, sliced jicama (a Latin American root vegetable), various salsas, guacamole and tortilla chips.

HOTTEST 7

makes 20 cakes; about 6 servings

2 ancho chili peppers, stemmed and seeded

2 chipotle chili peppers, stemmed and seeded

2 cups *masa harina* (Mexican cornmeal)

2 teaspoons dried chili powder

1 ½ teaspoons kosher salt

1 scant teaspoon baking powder

1 cup warm water

2 thick cayenne or Las Cruces chili peppers, stemmed, seeded, and minced

½ pound Monterey Jack cheese, finely grated

⅓ cup vegetable or peanut oil, for cooking

Sprigs of cilantro, for garnish

fiery east african vegetable and lentil stew

1 large onion, cut into dice

4 cloves garlic, finely chopped

4 bird's eye (Thai) or serrano chili peppers, stemmed and thinly sliced

1 1/2 tablespoons cayenne pepper

1 tablespoon *each* ground cumin and coriander seeds

1/2 teaspoon *each* ground cinnamon and cloves

4 tablespoons *ghee* or clarified unsalted butter (see note, page 53)

2 cups peeled, seeded, and chopped tomatoes

3/4 cup washed and sorted lentils

6 cups homemade vegetable stock (page 13) or canned vegetable broth (preferably low-sodium)

2 red potatoes, cut into dice

1 large carrot, cut into 1/2-inch pieces

2 cups tightly packed, washed and trimmed collard greens, cut into 1/4-inch strips

Salt and pepper, to taste

3 hard-cooked eggs, halved, for garnish

➤ This robust stew has so much body and flavor, not to mention nutritional value, even nonvegetarians will relish its deliciously hearty qualities.

HOTTEST 8

makes about 6 servings

In a large, heavy-bottomed pot, cook the onion, garlic, chili peppers, cayenne, cumin, coriander, cinnamon, and cloves in the *ghee* over moderate heat 5 to 7 minutes, stirring frequently. Add the tomatoes, lentils, and vegetable stock and bring to a boil over high heat. Reduce the heat to moderate and simmer 40 to 45 minutes, stirring occasionally, until the lentils are tender.

Add the potatoes, carrots, and collard greens and cook 12 to 15 minutes, or until all the vegetables are tender. Season with salt and pepper. Serve hot, garnished with the hard-cooked eggs.

baked polenta with chili peppers and smoked cheese

6 cups homemade vegetable stock (page 13) or canned vegetable broth (preferably low-sodium)

2 tablespoons unsalted butter

1¹⁄₂ cups coarse cornmeal

1 large California green or poblano chili pepper, stemmed, seeded, and finely chopped

3 red jalapeño or bird's eye (Thai) chili peppers, stemmed, seeded, and finely chopped

1 teaspoon cumin seeds

¹⁄₂ pound naturally smoked Cheddar or mozzarella cheese, finely grated

Salt and pepper, to taste

Vegetable oil, for brushing

Fresh herb sprigs, for garnish

➤ Team this delectable, chili-spiked polenta with a salad of lightly dressed mixed greens tossed with marinated artichoke hearts and green beans to make a well-rounded meal.

This recipe requires chilling the polenta for at least four hours before baking to allow it to set. If you don't have the time for this, you may eliminate the molding and baking steps and serve the polenta soft, spooned into a shallow bowl.

HOTTER 4

makes 8 servings

Lightly grease eight 1-cup molds or one 9-x-13-inch baking dish (for making diamond or square shapes).

In a large, heavy-bottomed saucepan, bring the vegetable stock and butter to a boil over high heat. Add the cornmeal, whisking constantly with a wire whisk for the first 5 to 7 minutes to form a smooth mixture. Reduce the heat to moderate and continue cooking, stirring constantly with a wooden spoon, 7 to 10 minutes or until the mixture is thick and smooth. Add the chili peppers and cumin and cook 7 to 10 minutes longer, stirring frequently, until very thick and aromatic.

Add the cheese, remove from the heat, and stir well until melted. Season with salt and pepper and immediately pour into prepared molds or a baking dish. (At this point, it may also be poured into a bowl and served soft.) Brush surface of polenta with a thin coat of vegetable oil and cover tightly with plastic wrap. Refrigerate for at least 6 hours or up to 24 hours.

Preheat oven to 400° F. Turn out polenta from individual molds and place on a large baking sheet or, if you used a 9-x-13-inch dish, cut polenta into 2-inch squares, rectangles, or diamond shapes and place on baking sheet. Bake 15 to 20 minutes, or until heated through and light golden brown. Serve immediately, garnished with fresh herbs.

potato-cheese tacos with three chilies

Preheat oven to 400° F.

Bake potatoes in center of oven 45 to 50 minutes, or until tender when pierced with a fork. Remove from oven and cool to room temperature. Slice in half and scrape the pulp into a large bowl; gently crumble with a fork. (Do not mash the potatoes or they will be gummy.)

To the potatoes add the cheese, chili peppers, egg, and cilantro; mix gently with a fork until thoroughly combined. Cover tightly with plastic wrap and refrigerate for 2 hours or up to 1 day.

To prepare tacos: Lay tortillas on a flat work surface. Using about 2 rounded tablespoons per tortilla, spoon the mixture onto one half of each tortilla. Fold over the second half and press gently to secure.

In a very large, nonstick sauté pan, heat about ¼ inch of oil over moderate heat until hot. Add as many tacos as will comfortably fit in the pan without crowding. Cook each side about 2 minutes, or until light golden brown and the filling is heated through. Remove with a slotted spatula and drain on paper towels. Cook the remaining tacos in this fashion, adding more oil as needed. Serve immediately, garnished with sprigs of cilantro.

➤ I find these vegetarian tacos irresistible and fun to eat.

Although they appeal to youngsters with adventurous palates, grown-ups will appreciate the homey ingredients and unique taste.

HOTTER 6

makes 4 to 6 servings

3 large baking potatoes (about 2¾ pounds)

⅓ pound sharp Cheddar cheese, finely grated

1 California green chili pepper, stemmed and finely chopped

3 red jalapeño chili peppers, stemmed, seeded, and finely chopped

1 hot goat horn or Hungarian sweet chili pepper, stemmed, seeded, and finely chopped

1 egg, lightly beaten

3 tablespoons minced fresh cilantro

10 to 12 6-inch corn tortillas

½ to ⅔ cup vegetable oil, for frying

Sprigs of cilantro, for garnish

frozen chocolate silk with ancho chilies

7-ounce jar marshmallow cream

3/4 cup corn syrup

2 teaspoons vanilla extract

1/3 cup cold water

1 envelope unflavored gelatin

2 cups half-and-half

8 ounces unsweetened chocolate, coarsely chopped

1 cup cocoa powder

4 toasted ancho chili peppers, stemmed, seeded, and ground, or 3 tablespoons hot chili powder

1/2 cup toasted peanuts, finely chopped (optional)

Fresh mint sprigs, for garnish

➤ This decadent frozen confection is sure to stimulate dinner conversation—if not your taste buds. The marriage of intense chocolate and dark, dusky ancho chili peppers makes an unforgettable combination. The garnish of toasted peanuts completes the Latin American character of this enchanting dessert.

HOTTER 4

makes about 6 servings

In a large bowl, using an electric mixer, beat the marshmallow cream, corn syrup, and vanilla until smooth. Set aside.

Place the water in a small bowl. Sprinkle the gelatin over the surface and let stand at room temperature 5 minutes. Stir well until dissolved. Set aside.

Place the half-and-half, unsweetened chocolate, cocoa powder, and ancho chili powder in a heavy-bottomed saucepan. Heat over moderate heat, stirring frequently, until chocolate has melted and mixture is thoroughly combined and smooth. Remove from heat, add the gelatin mixture, and mix well.

Add one third of the chocolate mixture to the marshmallow mixture; beat well until smooth. Add the remaining chocolate mixture and beat until thoroughly combined and smooth. Transfer to a storage container with a tight-fitting lid and place in freezer until set, about 6 hours. Remove 10 minutes before serving to soften slightly. Spoon into serving bowls and garnish with peanuts, if desired, and fresh mint. Serve immediately.

frijoles a los angeles con salsa a diablo • angelic beans with sauce of the devil

1 pound large lima beans, washed and sorted

2 ancho chili peppers, stemmed, seeded, and coarsely chopped

1 chipotle chili pepper, stemmed, seeded, and coarsely chopped

1 bay leaf

2 medium onions, coarsely chopped

16 habanero chili peppers, stemmed and coarsely chopped

3 red jalapeño or bird's eye (Thai) chili peppers, stemmed and coarsely chopped

6 cloves garlic, coarsely chopped

1 tablespoon *each* ground cumin and coriander

3 tablespoons olive oil

Salt and pepper, to taste

¹/₂ cup coarsely chopped fresh cilantro, for garnish

➤ The contrast between plump, mild-flavored white lima beans and their inferno-like sauce inspired the name for this blazing-hot bean dish. You may temper the heat by adding only half of the habanero chili peppers—which still guarantees a mouth-searing experience.

I like this dish with hot rolls spread with butter and drizzled with a little honey. You may also serve with warm corn tortillas or, for a more ample meal, cheese quesadillas made with flour tortillas.

HOTTEST 10+

makes about 8 servings

Soak the beans in 2 quarts water 8 to 12 hours, changing the water a couple of times during soaking. Drain beans in colander and place in heavy-bottomed, 8-quart saucepan. Add the ancho and chipotle chili peppers, bay leaf, and 5½ quarts of cold water. Bring to a boil over high heat, stirring frequently. Reduce heat to moderate and simmer 1½ hours, stirring occasionally.

In a very large sauté pan, cook the onions, habanero and jalapeño chili peppers, garlic, cumin, and coriander in the olive oil over high heat 5 to 7 minutes, stirring frequently. Using a large ladle, remove 2 cups of the bean cooking liquid and add to the onion-chili mixture. Cook 3 minutes, stirring constantly, until slightly thick. Remove from the heat, add 2 more cups of bean cooking liquid and cool slightly. Using a blender, purée the chili mixture in batches until nearly smooth. Add to the beans and mix well.

Cook the beans 45 to 50 minutes longer, stirring occasionally, until very tender. (If beans require still more cooking, add a little more water.) Season with salt and pepper. Serve garnished with cilantro.

INDEX

INDEX

TABLE OF EQUIVALENTS

The exact equivalents in the following tables have been rounded for convenience.

US/UK	METRIC
oz=ounce	g=gram
lb=pound	kg=kilogram
in=inch	mm=millimeter
ft=foot	cm=centimeter
tbl=tablespoon	ml=milliliter
fl oz=fluid ounce	l=liter
qt=quart	

◆ OVEN TEMPERATURES

FAHRENHEIT	CELSIUS	GAS
250	120	$1/2$
275	140	1
300	150	2
325	160	3
350	180	4
375	190	5
400	200	6
425	220	7
450	230	8
475	240	9
500	260	10

◆ WEIGHTS

US/UK	METRIC
1 oz	30 g
2 oz	60 g
3 oz	90 g
4 oz ($1/4$ lb)	125 g
5 oz ($1/3$ lb)	155 g
6 oz	185 g
7 oz	220 g
8 oz ($1/2$ lb)	250 g
10 oz	315 g
12 oz ($3/4$ lb)	375 g
14 oz	440 g
16 oz (1 lb)	500 g
$1^1/2$ lb	750 g
2 lb	1 kg
3 lb	1.5 kg

◆ LENGTH MEASURES

US/UK	METRIC
$1/8$ in	3 mm
$1/4$ in	6 mm
$1/2$ in	12 mm
1 in	2.5 cm
2 in	5 cm
3 in	7.5 cm
4 in	10 cm
5 in	13 cm
6 in	15 cm
7 in	18 cm
8 in	20 cm
9 in	23 cm
10 in	25 cm
11 in	28 cm
12 in/1 ft	30 cm

◆ LIQUIDS

US	METRIC	UK
2 tbl	30 ml	1 fl oz
$1/4$ cup	60 ml	2 fl oz
$1/3$ cup	80 ml	3 fl oz
$1/2$ cup	125 ml	4 fl oz
$2/3$ cup	160 ml	5 fl oz
$3/4$ cup	180 ml	6 fl oz
1 cup	250 ml	8 fl oz
$1^1/2$ cups	375 ml	12 fl oz
2 cups	1 l	32 fl oz

equivalents of commonly used ingredients

◆ ALL-PURPOSE (PLAIN) FLOUR/DRIED BREAD CRUMBS/CHOPPED NUTS

1/4 cup	1 oz	30 g
1/3 cup	1 1/2 oz	45 g
1/2 cup	2 oz	60 g
3/4 cup	3 oz	90 g
1 cup	4 oz	125 g
1 1/3 cups	6 oz	185 g
2 cups	8 oz	250 g

◆ WHOLE-WHEAT (WHOLE MEAL) FLOUR

3 tbl	1 oz	30 g
1/3 cup	2 oz	60 g
2/3 cup	3 oz	90 g
1 cup	4 oz	125 g
1 1/4 cups	5 oz	155 g
1 2/3 cups	7 oz	210 g
1 3/4 cups	8 oz	250 g

◆ WHITE SUGAR

1/4 cup	2 oz	60 g
1/3 cup	3 oz	90 g
1/2 cup	4 oz	125 g
3/4 cup	6 oz	185 g
1 cup	8 oz	250 g
1 1/3 cups	12 oz	375 g
2 cups	1 lb	500 g

◆ BROWN SUGAR

1/4 cup	1 1/2 oz	45 g
1/3 cup	3 oz	90 g
3/4 cup	4 oz	125 g
1 cup	5 1/2 oz	170 g
1 1/3 cups	8 oz	250 g
2 cups	10 oz	315 g

◆ RAISINS/CURRANTS/SEMOLINA

1/4 cup	1 oz	30 g
1/3 cup	2 oz	60 g
1/2 cup	3 oz	90 g
3/4 cup	4 oz	125 g
1 cup	5 oz	155 g

◆ LONG-GRAIN RICE/CORNMEAL

1/3 cup	2 oz	60 g
1/2 cup	2 1/2 oz	75 g
3/4 cup	4 oz	125 g
1 cup	5 oz	155 g
1 1/3 cups	8 oz	250 g

◆ ROLLED OATS

1/3 cup	1 oz	30 g
2/3 cup	2 oz	60 g
1 cup	3 oz	90 g
1 1/2 cups	4 oz	125 g
2 cups	5 oz	155 g

◆ DRIED BEANS

1/4 cup	1 1/2 oz	45 g
1/3 cup	2 oz	60 g
1/2 cup	3 oz	90 g
3/4 cup	5 oz	155 g
1 cup	6 oz	185 g
1 1/4 cups	8 oz	250 g
1 1/2 cups	12 oz	375 g

◆ JAM/HONEY

2 tbl	2 oz	60 g
1/4 cup	3 oz	90 g
1/2 cup	5 oz	155 g
3/4 cup	8 oz	250 g
1 cup	11 oz	345 g

◆ GRATED PARMESAN/ROMANO CHEESE

1/4 cup	1 oz	30 g
1/2 cup	2 oz	60 g
3/4 cup	3 oz	90 g
1 cup	4 oz	125 g
1 1/3 cups	5 oz	155 g
2 cups	7 oz	220 g